Dare to Believe

I am Healed

MARIE-JOSE MARDIROSSIAN

Contents

—❧✦☙—

Acknowledgments

J wanted to write this book as an encouragement to those cancer sufferers and families affected by this awful curse. I was diagnosed with Stage 4 cancer of the ovaries and colon. In my darkest days in hospital, I did not think I would get through the pain, but by God's grace and mercy, I am a survivor and living a life more pleasing to the Lord Jesus Christ.

A big thank you must go to my soulmate, Emil, my husband of nineteen years (aka the G.O.F—Grumpy Old Fart), to my elder triplet sister Jessica who has been by my side constantly. Last, but by no means least, my debt of gratitude also goes to the rest of my immediate family and extended family for their love, prayers, and support throughout. Not unlike Jacob, my family is quite extensive, so names are too innumerable to mention, but you know who you are.

Chapter One

The Early Years

$\mathscr{I}$ have known for as long as I can remember the love of the Lord Jesus Christ. I was very fortunate to be brought up in a loving household where morals and values were drummed into us from a very early age, and I was brought up in a Christian environment. In the '60s, life seemed a lot more manageable and easy, without so many of the hang-ups we find in society today. For example, I cannot remember facing the degree of pressure, as do today's children, to perform socially or academically among peers in particular and within society generally. The quote "winning isn't everything—it's the only thing!" didn't meant so much as today. The pressure for young adults to secure a job, along with owning their first home, has never been so great or unachievable as it is today. We seem to be chasing our tails just to keep still and to avoid being swept downstream by the current of ever increasing debt and bills, while the bare necessities of life seem to be ever more challenging to attain.

Moving on, and onto a more positive note; I am one of identical triplets. My triplet sisters' names are Jessica and Joy, and I am Jose. Of course, growing up you can imagine the confusion when letters arrived at the house addressed to Ms. J.

I have three older brothers, Patrick, Ian, and Bruce (no, they are not triplets!). How we triplets came into this world was a miracle only the Lord could have made with such humor. The Lord definitely has a sense of humor second to none. As my mom reminisces, one night my eldest brother prayed before bedtime, asking Jesus to let them each have a sister to play with. After leaving the bedroom, my parents looked at each other in shocked horror and said they hoped that was one prayer that would not be answered! Well, nine months later, out popped us triplets. Of course, in the '60s we were still pretty much in the dark ages when it came to baby scans, so my mom was only made aware that she was carrying triplets a month before she was due to deliver. Each of my brothers was allocated a sister to look after and keep amused while growing up. Even to this day, each one of us triplets has a close affinity to her "designated" brother.

We were brought up in South Africa, living in a large old house with an equally large garden. The struggle to feed six growing children spanning just four and a half years meant that money was always tight, but the love shown by my parents was immeasurable. My parents met in Holland when my mom was staying at my father's mother's B&B. I believe it was love at first sight, but then again, I'd rather not have to dwell on my parents' love lives! Soon after meeting, my father moved to South Africa and married my mom. Initially, after four years of marriage they did not think that they would be blessed with children, then the Lord's sense of humor kicked in, and they had six children under the age of four years and seven months. Also, they did not have TV in South Africa in the '60s, which helped.

Because identical triplets in the '60s were so rare, I am pleased to say we were definitely one in a million. My dad had to quickly come up with a solution as to how mom would feed us all at the same time, along with transporting us around together in strollers. Dad came up with an ingenious invention: a high chair that sat three of us in a row. Feeding time resembled a production line! The stroller consisted of two of us sitting in the front and one behind. It was a massive contraption but worked very well. The highchair was used for a number of other triplets in the area after us, so it served several families, and my dad's legacy lived on for a number of years thereafter.

My father had a very eventful life before he moved to South Africa. He fought for the underground forces in Holland during the Second World War and was the unofficial hairdresser for the underground men. Of course, with six children, his hairdressing skills were put to full use once again. Unfortunately, he would cut my brothers' hair first and then move onto us triplets. My father had become accustomed to cutting one style of hair, which suited men only. Despite our constant protests, we triplets were destined with identical cuts to my brothers for the next few years. It was definitely not the highlight of my childhood. We were so distraught after our haircuts that, on one occasion, we took matters into our own hands and gave each other a haircut one night. We found out the hard way that at the age of six, our hands were not steady enough, and we were left with fringes that ended half way up our crowns—hardly our finest hour, after which we left it to Dad to continue with the boy cuts!

Because we were such a large family, we did not really need friends, there were always enough kids around to play with in our large back garden. To be honest, my parents preferred to keep an eye on all six of us. Although, with six birthday parties a year, leading to sixty-plus children in the back garden every time, we didn't need to have friends around any more often. My father's skills extended to do-it-yourself (DIY) projects, and he built us a couple of tree houses in the back garden. I remember going to the circus once, and only once, as it was very expensive in those days. Instead, Dad built a few trapeze swings in the back garden as we really fancied our chances of joining the circus one day and becoming trapeze artists. However, we did not count on Joy breaking a front tooth when the swing hit her with the metal bar. As a result, we soon moved on from attempting to pursue a career as trapeze artists and instead decommissioned the old tennis court that was in the back garden and used it as a go-cart track with some old DIY cars. One day, we also decided to build a swimming pool. This was not to be just an ordinary pool, of course! This pool was to have a big section with a bridge where you could swim underneath and have a smaller pool on the other side. You are probably thinking of similar pools in exotic, not to mention exclusive, hotels. Well, you couldn't be more wrong! This was a mud pool, no walls, no tiles, and no filtration. Just the brute force Dad and we kids used to excavate the end of the back garden! When I look back I cannot imagine how dangerous it could have been if a mud slide took place. Clearly health and safety were not major issues in the '70s!

Another episode which springs to mind regarding health and safety, or rather the lack of, was when we were very young, my mom and dad had a light blue Ford Transit bus that used to be Africa's answer to the "von Traps" around town. My dad used to sit each one of us in turn on his lap while driving, and we used to think we were the King of the Castle. As for seat belts—what were they? My parents were constantly trying to please and amuse us in the most engaging ways possible, and we loved it.

My dad was twelve years older than my mom, but he insisted on acting the less mature, all for the sake of entertaining the family. I still remember him chasing us girls around the dining table, wearing his full, three-piece suit. He was also a very good cook and would always be working in the kitchen in a suit and apron. Being a gentleman, he insisted on standing up when a lady entered the room and was always the first to offer any help or assistance where required. He was what you would call a true gentleman.

I remember one day in winter when it was freezing cold and we were all complaining how cold we felt. Dad decided to show us some jumping exercises on how to keep warm, and he mentioned they used to do this back in Holland, where the weather was much colder than the winters in South Africa. One minute Dad was up in the air jumping and dancing, the next minute he was sprawled across the hallway floor in agony. He had twisted his ankle and could not move, much to everyone's amusement. He never did jump to keep warm again.

My dad was at one stage in his life a builder. He doubled the footage of our house with his bare hands. We triplets all shared a room with three iron beds all in a row, not dissimilar to an army barracks. The room was huge and had three built-in wardrobes and three built-in desks, as well. I remember one night we were jumping between the iron beds when I happened to slip and before long was sitting in the emergency room, nursing several stiches after a gallant effort to split my head open! These are all memories that tend to occupy your mind while lying in hospital with the hours dragging by.

Our house had a large dining table where the three boys sat on one side and us triplets on the other, with Mama Bear at one end and Papa Bear opposite. A lot of the time, meals were a kicking game. It would always be the triplets against the boys, always. We gathered very early on in life that power came in unity and therefore we triplets used to stick together against the boys. We always had competitions against the boys, including touch rugby and baseball. We definitely gave my brothers a run for their money. The other good thing was that we triplets used to be on the same netball team at school. Our team did very well in the school league, but to be honest, I think it was more that the opposition used to mix us up and go offside regularly, rather than our ball skills.

The other positive thing about being an identical triplet was that we could swap classes at school and no one would be the wiser. I was not particularly good at geography and would regularly swap classes with Jessica and vice versa. Of course, looking back, this was highly dishonest but was fun at the time—sorry Lord!

There is usually a negative as well to a positive; that is that being a triplet you were always blamed for something as a unit, even if you had nothing to do with it. It was always the "triplet's fault"; no one name was mentioned, just triplets. That used to annoy me, but the positives definitely outweighed the negatives. I am the middle triplet; Jessica is the eldest and Joy the youngest by a minute. What also used to annoy me was that in arguments, it would either come out "I'm the oldest, I should get it," or "I'm the youngest, I should get it." It would sound really silly if I said "I'm the middle ..." My mom and dad trusted in the Lord explicitly for all things. My dad had his own small business and, unfortunately, was made bankrupt by someone who absconded with his investment in a joint venture. Throughout this ordeal, and trying to support a family of eight, my father still kept the faith and kept tithing. How the Lord undertook and brought our family out of this financial ruin was a miracle, and throughout my growing up years there have been many instances where the Lord has intervened in miraculous ways that are unexplained; only Christ knows. More often than not, after a difficult ordeal, we always found ourselves in a far better place by God's grace.

In 1974, when I was six years old, I gave my heart to the Lord. I can vaguely remember the love of Christ and the warmth that filled my soul. We were at a young people's camping convention. In those days we did not have "glamping" like today. It was rain, mud, and firelight meals. It was a very precious time and a lot of innocent fun— something I will remember for the rest of my life. We used to run around in fields and supermarkets with bare feet and not worry how we looked; we cared just that we were happy and had no cares in the world. We triplets were definitely tomboys and would wear our brothers' hand-me-down clothes and did not care what people thought.

I remember that growing up, none of us children were given pocket money, but we were always provided with shoes and new sports equipment whenever we needed it. We grew up in an era where there was no TV—can you believe it! Black-and-white TV had just come to South Africa in the early '70s. I remember how we used to beg my father for a TV, including my mom. He was initially against having a TV in the house, but my poor father relented after all seven of us were at the neighbor's house on a regular basis—Billy no Mates springs to mind. I can remember thinking that we were the richest family in the neighborhood; we had a TV, and we could watch it at any time. My father did put his foot down, however, about having a VHS recorder in the house. His whole argument was that the kids needed to be outside playing and not in doors watching rubbish. I must say he did have a point, and I am forever grateful to Dad for sticking to his guns, though at the time I did think differently.

In a large household like ours we were constantly trying to find things to do. I think there is nothing worse than tirelessly complaining to parents, "I'm bored!" So, on school holidays and weekends we would often have cooking competitions: boys against the girls. We used to regularly hold pancake competitions in the house. It wasn't just how thin the pancakes were made, or what filling you used, but also how many you could eat. It wasn't just the cooking; it was definitely the eating competition afterward. At one stage, my mom thought we had worms because we all ate so much, so out came this horrid liquid we were all forced to swallow to deworm us.

As I mentioned earlier, we did not have much. Whenever sweets or cool drinks came into the house, it was up to Patrick, the eldest brother, to allocate even heaps of sweets to everyone. This included all six kids congregated around a table diligently counting each sweet in each pile. When it came to a cool drink, we would line up six glasses and ensure that the line of drink was even, not a millimeter more than the next glass. My excuse to this day is that I am making up for the lack of glucose I had as a child. It doesn't always work, but it makes me feel a lot better for it.

When it came to holidays we would usually go caravanning in the Katberg Mountains just outside our hometown. We used to go to the sunken round pool where all six of us used to go swimming in one direction to make a vortex in the pool. We would then swim in the opposite direction, and the sensation was great. Of course, being in the bush, we would come across all kinds of creepy crawlies, including snakes in the outhouse rafters. We would also ensure that we checked our clothes and shoes for any hidden scorpions or snakes before we got into them, too.

When we turned six years old, just after the self-inflicted haircuts, we all went on vacation to Holland. It did not pay, trying to look pretty and respectable for my dad's family, whom we had never met before. I remember my dad saving up for a long time to afford for the whole family to go overseas; it was definitely a holiday of a lifetime. I still remember that holiday—more so for the food we ate in Holland, rather that the specific sites. The enormous pancakes in the park were things of beauty I will never forget. Alkmaar and the amazing cheese market impressed me; I don't remember ever seeing so much cheese. It was also cherry season when we were there, and the abundance of cherries my uncle presented us with over a picnic was very special; we had never ever seen real cherries and so many of them. They were delicious. We were definitely spoiled rotten for three weeks in Holland by various uncles and aunts and enjoyed every minute of making new discoveries in a far-off land. I think that holiday burned into my memory so vividly that it would be some sixteen years later that Jessica and I would embark on a year-long stay in France. We had fantastic holidays when we were kids and ones I will treasure for the rest of my life. You definitely do not need a lot of money to have everlasting memories of childhood innocent fun and to know you are loved.

When it came to birthdays in the family, they would start very early in the mornings. Whichever birthday child it was would sit in my mom and dad's massive bed and the rest of us would come in with gifts, singing to them, and then all pile on top of the bed. The birthday boy or girl was then asked by my dad what they would like for dinner, and he would cook their favorite meal for them, while Mom would bake a birthday cake and treats. Growing up, Dad was the cook and Mom the baker. I don't know if it is a continental thing, but I find that in our house, I do the baking, and my husband does the cooking, of course, heavily supervised by me.

I mentioned earlier about how the Lord has intervened on many occasions in our lives while we were growing up. On one very memorable occasion it was New Year's Day. Now, New Years' Day in South Africa among the locals is much bigger and grander than Christmas. Our church was invited by one of the members to his safari park for the day, enjoying the animals and having a braai (aka barbecue). Of course, we were totally up for it. Growing up, their daughter was our best friend, and we would often find ourselves on a weekend up at the farm bareback horse riding, swimming, playing tennis and jumping on the trampoline—heaven. They also ran a hen hatchery called Gideon Hatcheries, where we could see how chicks were born right in front of our eyes—amazing. We took a couple of chicks home, and we called them Laurel and Hardy. They lasted a few months before we ate them—apologies for those people who believe they are pets.

On New Years' Day, we were all enjoying the fellowship and food when it was time to leave. We were told by a number of people to take the long way back home and not drive through the workers' huts as they would be drunk and looking for trouble. Needless to say, it was getting late, and my father thought nothing of the warning. We left in our blue Ford Transit with one car behind us in a little convoy, enjoying the open grassland. A few miles down the road, we came across half a dozen workers waving red flags. We naively thought that they were herding cattle or something. They were not; coming up closely behind them from the rise were a couple of hundred natives all drunk with machetes, knives, and sticks.

My father was very cool as he was in similar situations in Indonesia when he was a manager for the East India Company on one of their plantations, when the Hollanders were given forty-five minutes to leave Djakarta on the next boat out. So, we drove very slowly and calmly through the throng of people while they were rocking our van and making signs of slitting our throats. I don't think we have ever prayed so hard or fervently in our lives before. We really thought we would meet our Maker that day. The car behind us was honking for us to move quickly, but my dad told us to indicate to them to keep calm and go slowly and not show any fear. But by the grace of God, we got out of that situation and went directly to the local police station to report the incident. It happened that the throng had killed three supposed informers that day. It is a memory that will stick in my mind for the rest of my life, but, thank the Lord, I am here today to tell the tale.

I look back fondly on the "good old days." At school in our last couple of years, we triplets all took the same subjects: shorthand/typing. We had the old typewriters where the bell used to ring towards the end of the right-hand side of the page, and you would have to slam the carriage-return handle to start a new line. Surprisingly, we also had to use our brains to work out the center of the page and margins on one page and two. No calculators were allowed in those days; everything was driven by brainpower. To be honest, none of us triplets passed mathematics as math was the pain of our lives. Even at secretarial college—we all went to the same one—we all failed math. Bruce and Patrick, qualified accountants, had the brains and tried to explain the basics of accounting/administration to us, but to no avail. My dad always said that my brothers had the brains and the triplets had his legs. Trust me, it was a compliment. My dad played semi-professional football back in Holland, and he had some awesome legs. We were more interested in sports than math in those days, but of course, we regretted later in life that we did not concentrate more on our studies. But we enjoyed it while it lasted.

We had a very stern teacher called Miss Hall who was about one hundred years old and very strict "old school." She used to cover our keyboards, walk around with a ruler, and if anyone was sneaking a peek at the keys, they would have their knuckles wrapped. I have very fond memories of my school years, especially spending time with my sisters as a unit against the rest of the world.

We triplets all went to secretarial college in Port Elizabeth after school and enjoyed the year very much. I am grateful for the work ethic and values instilled in me during school and college—they definitely don't seem to make secretaries like they used to. I may be a little biased in saying this.

Chapter Two

Work Life

—❦—

From a very early age, my parents encouraged each one of us to be self-reliant and to find part-time jobs while we were still at school. They wanted to instill in us the value of hard work for our money. I found a job in a local, well-known Irish bakery called Shamrock Bakery. I worked every weekend and holidays in the bakery front and also in the back for five years and enjoyed every minute of it. When Easter came around, I was in the back baking hot cross buns; when Christmas hit, it was mince pies for Africa! This is probably where I found my love of baking and eating lovely cakes. When the bakery staff went on strike, my boss, Mr. Ryan, used to park outside our house, and I would sneak out of our bedroom window and work from midnight to 8:00 a.m. baking lovely bread and filling jam donuts and cream pastries—yum. I would be dropped off and have to knock on the bedroom window for one of my sisters to open the window so I could sneak back in by the time my parents woke up. Sorry, Mom; you did not know this until now! Every Saturday afternoon when the bakery closed for the weekend, all the staff was given the baked goods that were not sold that day. Invariably, when I got home there was the family waiting for me to open the bags full of lovely delights. My favorite treat was the Cornish pasties, and Shamrock bakery was very well known for their pies and pasties. They were very fattening but very satisfying.

After graduating from college with my sisters, Jessica and I moved to France for a year to work as au-pairs. Jessica was stationed in Paris, and I was in Saulieu, Burgundy. It was a fantastic experience as no one could speak English in the small village, so it forced me to become pretty fluent in French; otherwise I would have starved. I worked for a well-known three-star Michelin Chef. To be honest, being so green from my little hometown, I had no idea what that meant. It was a fantastic year as I stayed in the hotel for the duration of my stay and ate the very finest food. It was the first opportunity I had to drink very nice wine and eat amazing cheeses that I had never tasted before. Back in South Africa, due to the sanctions, we did not have the variety of cheese or meats that I discovered in France; it was a real eye opener. The whole experience, looking back, was amazing, and I am sorry I never cherished each moment like I should have. I also loved playing tennis at the local tennis courts and won the local tennis league in the village and went to Roland Garros with the chef's wife and got to sit in the Presidential Box. I was in a fortunate position that the husband was always busy in the restaurant, so the wife would take me with her to some lovely events I could have only dreamt of.

It was a surreal experience in a lot of ways. I got to meet a lot of the Monaco royal family when they flew in for a meal at the hotel. Also, I met Francois Mitterrand; for those of you who are too young to remember, he was a past president of France. Also a number of well-known French singers and actors came to the hotel. Of course I did not have a clue who they were, but everyone else seemed to be in awe.

Every Sunday was my day off, although it did not end up like that. However, I did make an effort to go to the local Catholic Church in the mornings. I initially did not understand a word of what was going on in the service, but later on during the year I got the hang of the French language.

I remember one morning early in the year, before I had a chance to learn much French that I was asked by a group of people from the kitchens if I wanted to do "elastic fun." I, of course, jumped at the chance just to get a break from hotel life. It wasn't until five hours into the road trip that I started worrying. In my mind I interpreted "elastic fun" as trampolines, and I was wondering why we were spending five hours in the car, driving to a venue that provided trampolines. It wasn't, however, until we turned a corner in Grenoble that we came across a bridge and it dawned on me; it was bungee jumping. I don't think I have ever been so scared in my entire life—ever! I could not back out, but I was petrified. I remember the instructors running through some rules and me having to sign my life away. While cuing up to do the jump, there was a rather large gentleman in front of me. I made the excuse to him that I was nervous and needed to jump as soon as possible. Little did he know that I was more terrified that his weight would stretch the elastic, and I would hit my head on the ground below! I was therefore determined to jump before him; fortunately he let me go first—whew! Ever since the dreaded bungee jump, I have been scared of heights and, of course, flying. I know it is ridiculous, but I still have a vague memory of having to dive off this very high bridge and bouncing backwards and forwards, definitely not something for the faint hearted, and I will certainly not do another one again.

Hotel life was amazing, and I made very good friends with everyone. Once the chefs had finished their evening shifts, we used to have midnight snacks of fondues and crepes. Some of the chefs working in the kitchens even paid my employer to work for him—can you believe it? I definitely tried new foods, including frogs' legs, which were delicious. I remember the sommelier, Lionel, had a huge nose and reminded me of a cartoon character. I have to say that while living in the hotel, I did miss "normal" food. It was so hard to come by regular baguettes, and I craved them. The hotel only offered walnut bread and various other artisan breads—but no boring, white, stodgy, everyday bread. I used to sneak out with the little girl I looked after, Berangere, and we used to buy plain white bread and other little treats without the parents knowing. She and I were like two naughty school kids in the middle of a field, eating forbidden fruits; it was lovely. We also used to forage blackberries and blueberries on wild hedge rows and chase the birds. I have to say it was sometimes difficult getting blackberry and chocolate stains out of our clothes before getting back to the hotel.

The little girl I looked after was beautiful, and I fell in love with her straight away. I remember my dad warning me before I left South Africa that I must not fall in love with my charge, but of course it is hard not to, and I was heartbroken when I left France. She used to be with me 24/7 as her parents were very busy with the business. I felt very sorry for her as I would have to wake the little girl up and dress her in matching dresses and hats all by Dior or Yves St Laurent when TV crews and photographers came around. It was certainly another world I was living in that year and an experience I am unlikely to forget.

At the end of the year we spent in France, Jessica and I moved back to little old East London, South Africa. After experiencing the big wide world, it was very difficult not to want to go back out and see more of life and the world. Don't get me wrong; East London is absolutely beautiful. It is on the East Coast of South Africa between Port Elizabeth and Durban with white sandy beaches like you only dream of, and a slow pace of life. Jessica and I had the travel bug and wanted to explore the big wide world, and we knew that finding a job in South Africa was going to be tough. Jessica and I decided to move to England as we could at least speak and write the language fluently. By this time my other sister, Joy, had married and was living a very happy life back home, but we did miss her terribly.

When we arrived in England, we moved to a one-bedroom rented room and started temping straight away. The two years we had temped stood us in good stead for the years ahead in the competitive workforce of London. My very first job was as a secretary at Nestle in the marketing department, and I thoroughly enjoyed the very busy pace of work. Of course, I enjoyed the staff shop even more! I was fortunate enough to temp a couple of long stints in Croydon before moving to the *big* city of London. My first job in the city was as office manager cum secretary in a ship brokering company in the Aldwych in London. This is where I met my future husband. It was amazing, looking back how God had a plan for us to meet—it was love at first sight (for me anyway; my husband took a bit longer convincing!). My husband is Armenian, and his first twelve years of life was spent in Iran before his family immigrated to England. I still am in awe that here he was from Armenia; I am from South Africa and we met up in London—God is amazing. I then left the company after nine months as it was a very small company and relationships were frowned upon.

I then moved to Standard Bank, a South African-owned investment bank, working as a Personal Assistant on the trading floor. It was nice to get back to working in a South African environment, with the unique sense of humor of the South African employees. The workforce consisted of roughly 40 percent South African, so it was home away from home. I worked there for twelve years before I decided to move on to bigger and better things. I still keep in contact with my ex-boss for a cup of coffee and have very fond memories of my tenure at the bank. The good thing was that my boss took me along with him to various departments where we would do a "clean up" and then move to the next department. Finally, he became CEO, and I was fortunate enough to be with him for the last three years of my career at Standard Bank. This stood me in good stead for future jobs because I learned a lot— particularly how to multi-task. Standard Bank was by far the busiest job I have had in my career, and while I was a young spring chicken, it was good.

I then moved to AON Insurance. I am sure everyone knows AON by the Manchester United football shirts and not as the world's largest insurance broker. The funny thing is, I have heard people think that Aon was an energy company—no comment! How the Lord found me the job so quickly was amazing, and I had the nicest Australian boss ever, to work for. How that came about was a miracle in itself. I was hired to work for the CEO, who then left after six weeks in the job and transferred to Bermuda. I then got my new boss, and I could not have wished for a nicer, more humble person to work for. He moved back to Australia after his two-year contract expired, and I left out of loyalty. I trusted the Lord explicitly to find me another job that would be fulfilling and where I could make an impact to His glory. Throughout my career, I have always leaned on Him to open or close doors and give me the job where He wants me, and He has never failed me yet.

After two months of looking for a job I was, to be honest, getting quite desperate. Fully trusting in the Lord who never fails, He found me my next job in a most miraculous way. A week before leaving Aon, my boss had a visitor from another insurance company who came to meet with him. We got to chatting beforehand, and the visitor mentioned in passing that I should forward my resume to him as he has some contacts in the business. Little did I know that he would be forwarding it to his daughter, who works in human resources in a well-known insurance company in the city of London. She passed my resume on to her ex-boss, who had started a start-up insurance company, and was looking for a PA. Out of the blue, I got a call at home from "an American gentleman," asking if I would meet him at Starbucks for a chat. I met him and liked him straight off. To cut a long story short, I was offered the job on the spot and signed on the dotted line within a couple of days. I really did not expect a job offer when I went to meet him. I just thought he wanted to pick my brain about the market and so forth.

I spent a good two years in that job and thoroughly enjoyed myself, and in the process, made a good friend. Unfortunately, it seems a pattern emerging and I am not taking it personally; my boss moved back home to Miami, and I therefore resigned and started looking for another job. We still keep in touch and meet for coffee or dinner when he is in town.

The Lord has truly blessed me throughout my two previous jobs. After leaving both jobs, I was given six month's pay by each employer and had great recommendations from them both. This stood me in good stead for my next job.

Looking for my next job was stressful, and it took a lot of faith to trust in the Lord to find it—and He did, as always. A couple of weeks out of a job, I went for an interview at a private school; I was offered the job, but I did not feel it was right for me. To start off with, I had to call my new boss Headmaster, and not by his name—that was totally not me. In all my jobs, I have wanted a good relationship with my new boss, where we could have a laugh but also get the job done. I am not into etiquette and just love being myself, with no airs and graces. I politely declined.

I then had no interviews for a month before I went for an interview at another insurance company. They seemed to like me after the second interview but were stalling on making a decision. In the interim, I went for an interview with a prestigious private equity company in the city. I liked the fact that its location was very close to the train station, and it was a very small boutique firm. Unfortunately, I did not get the job I was going for and was bitterly disappointed, but I knew that God had a plan—although, sometimes I wish He would share it! However, a month later I got a call back from the private equity firm to say that another job had come up and if I was interested, they would love me to come in and see a couple of the Managing Directors. I went in and liked them instantaneously and knew that it was the right place for me to be. The two MDs were quiet and reserved but sincere, and the team of associates was young and dynamic.

However, a curve ball was thrown when the insurance company also offered me the job at the same time. I prayed about it and decided to go with the private equity company, and it is a decision that was the best decision I have made in my career. It is just amazing to think that the Lord is interested in my well-being—little, insignificant me. It says in the Word that before time began my life was in His hands. He knows my thoughts; He knows my every move and hears me when I call. The creator of the universe cares so much for me; he even knows how many hairs are on my head—Wow!

For sixteen months prior to my diagnosis, I worked diligently at the firm and got to know everyone really well as there is only a total of ten staff in the London office. When I first joined, the associates and MDs were quite focused and had not much time for small talk. They used to walk into the office and walk straight past my desk, rushing off to begin their workday to make conference calls, attend meetings, and travel all over the globe. I remember wondering, after my three-month probation, what I was doing in such an environment. I knew God had a plan for me, He put me here for a reason, but I just did not know what. I have always been someone who goes through the workday very friendly and quite loud but balances that with a diligent and supportive work ethic. I have seldom taken myself seriously, and I think the various bosses I have had have appreciated my down-to-earth approach. It took a few months to find my feet and to get used to the work environment.

As soon as my work colleagues heard about my illness, I cannot explain to you how overwhelmed I was with their generosity and support. Religiously, every three weeks, a couple of my work colleagues would visit me at home, and whenever I was in the hospital, I had a crowd of them around my sickbed. I have been absolutely blown away by everyone's care, love, concern, and patience during this illness. I can honestly say we are like family now, and if anything happens to one of us, they know that I am praying for them and that the team is behind them.

How the Lord looks after his children has been eye-opening to me, and I am in absolute awe of Him who provides for my every need. After my diagnosis, I was concerned about my job, and also, of course, our finances, as we could not afford for me not to work. By God's provision and wonderful grace, the owner of the company made sure my salary was fully paid every month and told me to take things easy and just heal and get better and that my job was waiting for me. Thank you, Lord!

I just could not imagine this kind of generosity anywhere else in the workplace. The Lord is my provider, and I thank Him for all his blessings day by day. I put all my burdens onto Jesus and knew full well that He cared for me. "Fear doubts the Lord Jesus" is so easy to say, but actually believing it has brought a whole new meaning and deeper understanding of this.

Don't get me wrong, throughout my life I have been sorely tested by the devil. People need to understand that there is spiritual warfare going on around us. We cannot see it, but we know it exists and is real. The devil seeks out those people who choose to listen to him. Are you listening folks—we can either choose to believe the devil and his wicked lies or choose to believe the great I AM, who only wants good things for us.

The only power the devil has over us is lies, deceit, and cunning; he is like an annoying bug that is at people's minds, going on and on and on about things which are absolute rubbish. We need to know when to squash that annoying bug and tell him where to go. Our God is a good God; and only good, wholesome, honest, true things come from Him who made us, and loves us, and died for us, and who is waiting for us in glory.

I have had moments lying prostrate on the floor at home crying gut-wrenching cries from the very depths of my soul. I have felt so lost and hopeless and full of despair, not knowing how to get out of certain situations. I have had very low moments, pleading with God to help me!

I can honestly say He has helped in some miraculous ways throughout my life. I can imagine one day being in heaven and seeing all my tears in a glass vase, but next to my glass vase is another even bigger glass vase—those are the tears of my Lord Jesus Christ. You see, I know that Jesus is with me through the toughest, darkest moments of my life, carrying me through. He is someone I can lean on and put my hand in His hand while He shows me that there is a way out. The peace and joy that floods my very soul after one of my crying sessions is immense. I feel as if I have been at the very feet of Jesus, laying my head in His lap and Him stroking my hair and telling me how much He loves me and that everything is going to be alright.

Thank God I have not had that many crying sessions, but when I do, I think the whole of the United Kingdom can hear!

Chapter Three

My Diagnosis

*I*n 2009, as a background to all of this, my sister Jessica developed breast cancer. At the time, it was a huge shock, as we were all so healthy. At such a young age, we never thought it would affect us. Jessica had a mastectomy and reconstruction at the same time. As you can imagine, she was unable to do much for six months— no lifting things, and so forth. She had the most amazing network of friends and church members looking after her at this time. One lady in particular, Debbie, moved in with Jessica and literally looked after her solidly for the six months she was off work. At the time, Jessica said that if anyone in the church was ever affected by cancer, she would look after them as well as she had been looked after. Not surprisingly, years later, Jessica did not think it would be her sister!

Another thought that only hit me after my diagnosis, and what I had said at the time of Jessica's diagnosis was that "God forbid I ever get cancer, but if I do, let it be a surprise." I said that because I saw how painful the biopsy was for Jessica. They took tissue from her breast while she was still awake as you are not allowed to have a general anesthetic—apparently this was the most painful thing ever. Also, the stress of waiting for the biopsy results to see if it was or was not cancer, was unbearable. I am such a coward; I did not want to go through all that uncertainty. God was faithful in this, and I cannot thank Him enough.

In April, 2013, I started noticing a change in—sorry to be so crude—my bowel movements. I made an emergency appointment with the doctor's office down the road from our house. The nurse examined me and then called a doctor in for a second opinion. He felt my tummy and both recommended a laxative and told me not to worry as it seems like constipation. I was quite relieved to hear that, although the pain was intense. I had to trust the superior knowledge of the doctor and nurse.

For the next couple of months, things seemed to have improved slightly but not much. I then went for another emergency appointment in June as I was getting worried about "my movements." The nurse examined me and suggested I take laxatives, and it should clear itself; there was nothing to worry about, just a blockage. At the back of my mind I knew something was wrong, but thought I may be a drama queen, as the doctors and nurses know what is best. If they are saying it is constipation, then I should move on.

In the evening of Tuesday, July 9, I asked my husband to call the ambulance as the pain was unbearable. He called 911 and gave a run through of my symptoms. After ninety minutes with no-show, we decided to cancel the ambulance, pray and try and get some sleep. That night I was very sick, and I had no control of my bowel movements. Basically, the bathroom was a sanctuary for me, and I could not see an end to the pain I was in. I have never in my life experienced such pain, and at one stage I just wanted to die. I can imagine it being like childbirth, but for weeks on end with no resolution. I was seriously getting desperate for the pain to just stop. I woke up with pain, I went to work with pain, and I went to sleep with pain. I could just not see a way forward from there; I was desperate.

It was on Wednesday, July 10, when I made my third emergency appointment to the doctor's office. By this time, my tummy was distended, and I was in a lot of pain. The nurse looked at me and said that I should not take Movicol but recommended Fybogel. As some people may know, Fybogel is a form of laxative which is wheat based and hardens and expands bowel movements. After seeing the nurse, I went to the pharmacy and bought a box of Fybogel. I took one of the sachets and nearly died from the pain. At this stage I was still thinking that I may be a bit of a drama queen, and I should get over this constipation and move on.

All during that week, I was still going to the gym in the mornings and working a full day at the office. It was unbelievably painful and very hard to get through. Once I was caught putting my head on the desk out of sheer pain and not knowing how to get through the day. I just wanted to curl up and die.

Early on Thursday, July 11, I called the doctor's office and made yet another emergency appointment. I went to the gym at my usual time, 6:00 a.m. but had no energy to do anything but have a shower. I went to the office early to clear emails and then went for the emergency appointment at 9:20 a.m. When I got to the doctor's office, who should I see but the nurse from the previous day. The first thing she said to me was "you again!" That did not encourage me one bit, and I felt really bad about inconveniencing the doctor again. I begged her to get my doctor in, as something was terribly wrong.

Thank the Lord, my doctor was called in, and she noticed straight off how distended my tummy was and what pain I was in—I looked six months pregnant. She fortunately called the ambulance to take me to emergency room. I can't tell you how grateful and reassured I was that finally something was going to be done with my condition. I quickly called my husband on my cell to say that the ambulance was on its way and was taking me to the ER and asked if he could meet me there with an overnight bag. I thought, worse case, they would keep me overnight at the hospital for observation or something. When the ambulance came, within minutes, I was a bit embarrassed and apologized for the inconvenience of calling them out. I had never been in an ambulance before, let alone have the lights and siren going—very exciting. If I was not in such pain, I would have enjoyed the ride a lot more.

In the ambulance, being a bit over the top on tidiness, I tried to get my shoes off before lying down on the clean white sheet, which was on the stretcher. It's funny to think back on that, but I was always insisting on people taking shoes off when they come to my house and was always trying to keep things as I found them. Fortunately, I was told that it wasn't necessary to take my shoes off as they put a clean sheet on the stretcher after every call, which was reassuring. Also, I really do not think I could have managed bending over to take my shoes off and getting up again. They gave me gas and air in the ambulance, which was most helpful, and they asked on a scale of 1–10 what my pain was. I really wasn't trying to be clever, but I said it was 11. The pain was unbearable at this stage, especially lying down. I found myself moaning and groaning without meaning to, but the relief of getting some sort of help was so amazing that I felt like crying.

When we arrived at the emergency room I was fortunately wheeled right in and given morphine. If anyone has had morphine, they will know that it is incredibly sweet. Thank goodness, I did not know at the time that morphine is actually rat poison! I saw a young, good looking doctor, which always helps the pain relief! Don't worry; he was young enough to be my son. They did various scans and took blood samples from me before wheeling me down to have a CT scan. Until then, the blood and urine samples were all normal.

My husband, Emil, finally arrived at the emergency room with my overnight bag in his hand. It was a relief to see him, as things were moving so fast. I was slightly out of it, what with all the morphine and drugs the emergency room staff were plying me with, just to ease the pain. I was then wheeled up to one of the hospital wards to settle in and be comfortable, and wear one of the sexy hospital gowns. Everything was such a blur for me on the one hand; on the other hand I was very excited. I had never been in hospital since I was a young child; everything was new. I was just very relieved they had a bed for me, and I was been looked after now. All this time I was praying that the blood of Jesus cover me, His love enfold me, and His will be done with whatever is happening.

Shortly afterward, I was told that they would be operating on me that night. Needless to say, I was surprised that things were progressing that fast, but I was pleased to see they were taking me seriously. I felt huge relief that I really was not being a drama queen. I was surprised that I needed to be operated on so quickly; what happens normally when someone is diagnosed with constipation? I envisaged a needle been pricked into my tummy and everything just deflates like a balloon and gets back to normal, or something.

I was wheeled down to surgery at around 7:00 p.m. that night. All I remember was praying that the Lord's will be done and that whatever happens, He is in control. I then had to count to 10—I managed 3—before I went under.

I heard weeks later that Emil stayed outside the operating theater from 7:00 p.m. to midnight that evening during the whole operation, with hourly reports from one of the team. Emil was briefed by the surgeon afterward and was told that they had successfully removed everything benign and malignant they could see, including a half meter of colon—I did not realize I had so much to give!

All I remember is waking up the next morning in ICU. I thought I had visions during the night of two angels at the end of my bed, overseeing the monitors and my progress, and they had a clipboard in their hands. Angels or nurses, I was well looked after, except for the bleeping monitors everywhere. I was happy until I looked down at my bandaging and a couple of bags stuck to my tummy. I was not sure what the bags were for and was too weak to ask.

Later that morning in ICU, I had a visit from a nurse dressed in maroon who was coming to change one of my bags. I was still not sure what she was going to do until she took off the bag, and I saw this "thing" sticking out of my tummy. I had heard of a colostomy before but never appreciated what they were. Needless to say, I was in shock. At forty-five years of age, I felt like an old person; surely only old people have colostomies! I have learned since then that that is not true, but you only know of these things once you have it yourself. My other bag was for drainage, which was thankfully temporary. It drained fluid from my colon after the operation and was in me for only five days. I just felt like a cow with two udders stuck to me—not a pretty sight.

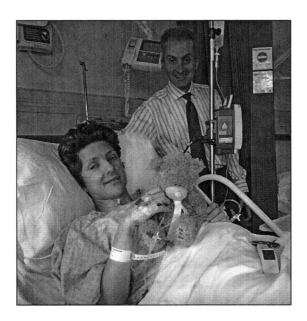

I then remembered years back how I commented that "God forbid, I ever get cancer, let it be a surprise." Well, God was merciful and so very thoughtful to little me; I am amazed by His goodness. I had no biopsies, no guessing is it or isn't it; nothing like that. If I knew that I would have to have a colostomy and prepare for the operation, I don't think I could have handled it. For me, this was the best-case scenario—although I would have preferred not to get cancer at all. Satan definitely, in these last days, is seeking to kill and destroy the people of faith—those who believe in the Lord Jesus Christ. Thank God, I plan to run this race and finish this race to His glory.

I then received a visit from my surgeon who quickly went through what he had done the night before in surgery. That was the first time I heard that I had tumors in my left ovary which they removed, and a nine-centimeter tumor blocking my colon. I was told that I could have died within twenty-four hours if I had not been treated, as the tumor could of exploded inside. I was speechless; I really was not able to say anything except cry; the shock was too much. I went from thinking that I had a bad case of constipation to having actual ovarian and colon cancer, and it was shocking.

I then rang Emil and told him what the surgeon had said. Of course, he was in shock as well. Although the surgeon spoke to him after the operation the previous night, he did not register cancer; all he was concerned about was that they removed whatever needed removing and I was alive—bless him. He came straight over to the hospital, and by Friday lunchtime, I was moved back to the ward I initially went into the previous night. I had to laugh as I saw the overnight bag sitting on the chair next to my bed—I realized I would be in hospital a lot longer than I initially thought.

I did not know until afterwards that one of the ICU nurses had called my sister and told her to come to the hospital as I had just received some bad news. It was a relief to see Jessica and her husband at my bedside. We spent the whole of Friday just chatting, between my nodding off. I was at peace with everything and with all the prayers going on around my bed—I was in a good place. The "peace that passeth all understanding" was with me. Okay, the morphine helped, as well.

On Saturday, I had a visitor from the chaplaincy come to visit as she was doing her rounds. She was an amazing lady, and I could tell she was filled with the Holy Spirit. I just cried when I saw her and starting talking about the goodness of the Lord Jesus, and how that I am alive talking to her was a miracle. She then asked if I would like breaking of bread on Sunday at my bed. Of course, I jumped at that. The more normal things I had around me the better. Especially in a hospital ward, seeing all the sick people around, I needed to be covered by the blood of Jesus and by his grace and mercy. Within my spirit I was absolutely fine; I still did not think I was ill and just wanted to get back to as normal a life as possible. Being in hospital was still a dream to me; it did not feel real being here.

On Saturday, my poor sister and her husband, along with Emil, tried to keep things as normal as possible back at the house. My brother-in-law is a landscape gardener, so he kindly put everyone to work and trimmed the hedges, tidied the beds, and all the OCD (over the top) gardening stuff we used to do at our house. They brought pictures of the finished tidied garden to show me what they had done that day. I was so grateful and remembered how hot it was outside—they must have burned a few calories doing it.

Sunday came, and at 10:00 a.m., a lovely lady missionary came to visit. The little service she gave was sweet but very much traditionally based, but all the same, full of God's love. She then gave me a beautiful little carved crucifix for me to keep. I can't tell you how many early mornings and late nights I would lie awake and hold the crucifix in my hands and pray and worship and honor the Lord Jesus for his goodness. If it was not for Him, I would definitely not have had the joy of the Lord as my strength throughout my hospital stay.

The morning service must have been really exhausting for me as I slept all afternoon and missed my sister's visit. The nurses told her not to interrupt me as I had not slept the night before. I still cannot remember how long I slept, but it was the first time I had a proper deep sleep—it was lovely.

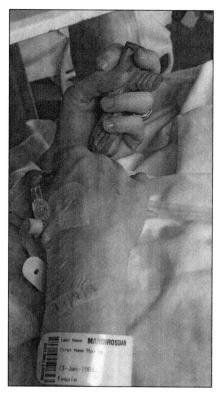

I am generally a very light sleeper, and of course in hospital, I was worse than ever. Because of all the bags stuck on my tummy, I had to lie on my back. A few years ago I was in a car accident in the United States and had a bad case of whiplash. My back had never recovered, and, therefore to this day, I am unable to lie on my back for long periods of time. As a result I would lie in hospital sleeping in a seated position, which was not ideal or comfortable.

I would play with the buttons on the side of the hospital bed and put the bed up to a seating position as far as it would go. So, I ended up talking and praying to the Lord all night, every night, and that was a truly blessed time for me to embrace God's grace and feel his love enfolding me. I used to hold the crucifix up to the outside light and just focus on the outline of the cross and dwell on His suffering and how much He gave for me. Then I realized that what I was going through was nothing compared to the agony of the cross.

On Sunday, my sister Jessica and her husband left to go back to Essex where they lived. On Monday, she came back and spent the next three weeks looking after me. She spent the Monday to Thursday visiting me in hospital and reading the scriptures to me and just talking about girlie stuff—it was great. She will never know how much she meant to me and what a boost she was to my morale. In fact, Jessica was a blessing to everyone in the ward. By that time, I had become friendly with the ladies in the ward and Jessica as well. Jessica would help plump their pillows, get drinks for the ladies, and generally do their running around for them. She was definitely God's light shining in that ward. I also found myself some mornings reading the daily devotional to the ladies. I am still not too sure what they thought of it, but no one stopped me, which is always a good sign.

As Christians we need to be bold. We need to be vessels on earth whereby the Lord can work through us. God's light needs to shine through us to the outside world, whereby we can give a message of hope and love to a lost world. I am always amazed how many people are very open and willing to hear the good news, the gospel of our Lord Jesus Christ. What a privileged position I find myself in, being able to spread the love of God to ladies in the ward who are desperate for a message of hope.

A song I often find myself singing is:

My hope is built on nothing less, than Jesus'
blood and righteousness.
On Christ the solid rock I stand;
all other ground is sinking sand.
My hope is Jesus—the anchor of my soul,
the ruler of the universe,
The One Who's in control. He saved me,
and He will keep me until the end.
The rock of my salvation—on Christ I will depend.
My hope is Jesus.

Chapter Four

Hospital Holiday Camp

For the next 5 days was pretty much a blur. Between morphine, antibiotics, and various other drips and drains, I don't remember much. I was fortunate enough to be at the end of the ward overlooking the outside, so I had a window seat. All I do remember is that the antibiotic drip made me incredibly sick, but other than that all seemed well considering.

After five days, my catheter was removed, which was a big event for me at the time and meant independence; I could freely walk myself to the toilet—hooray! It was at this time that the nurses threatened me with feeding me intravenously if I did not start eating. The last thing I wanted was to have another injection, so that definitely gave me the motivation to eat. I remember my first meal. I requested mashed potatoes—bad mistake! It came to me looking like cardboard glue; it was not appetizing despite the copious amounts of pepper I put on it. After that meal, I consciously made an effort to get out of bed and start walking. This was the first time I actually got motivated and determined to recover as soon as physically possible—with God's help, of course. What I did not want to happen was to start feeling sorry for myself and wallow in my sorrow. I thought back on Lance Armstrong: how he had made a full recovery after his cancer and how he had programed his body to be unique and perfect for cycling—okay, with the help of drugs, as well. I wanted to be the same, get back to normality, walk and eat a lot, and build up my strength. I was determined not to be a victim. I wanted my life and body back to normalcy as soon as physically possible, the way God intended.

I met some lovely ladies in the ward I was staying in. The lady opposite me was called Iris, and she was eighty-nine years old. She weighed only 84 lbs, and she was beautiful inside and out. She had broken a bone in her neck from falling out of bed in her nursing home, so she had already spent a good three weeks in the ward when I arrived. The two weeks I ended up staying in hospital were the hottest days of the summer. We had no rain, and I remember wishing, what with my window seat, that I could see some rain. Unfortunately, it did not happen. Poor Iris had this massive neck brace on her in the heat of the summer, sweltering like a bud in the corner of the ward. I would help her put her fan on during the day just to try and keep her cool. I definitely had a soft spot for little Iris and still wonder how she is doing. Iris was discharged a day after me back to her son and daughter-in-law's care.

The lady next to me was called Gillian. She had been in a hit-and-run accident, and as a result had broken both arms. I felt really sorry for her; she was unable to drink or feed herself at all. Gillian was in the hospital for the same amount of time as Iris was when I came on board. I remember Gillian and I encouraging little Iris to eat, and Iris and I would have eating competitions who would finish their plates of food. Iris was fed these energy and calorie boosting drinks in small bottles. They gave me one initially to drink, but they were absolutely disgusting. This was another motivating factor for me to get up and eat proper food.

Jessica had lent me her iShuffle to listen to some of her music and I, in turn, had lent mine to Iris. Iris loved jazz and classical music, so I would play her some of her favorite music; she loved that. A couple of nights, I would tuck the two ladies away at night, cover them with their blankets, and pray good night to them both. Considering my diagnosis, I felt strong and able to comfort others, thanks to the Lord God for his mercies and love.

The routine in the hospital was relentless. Every morning we would be served breakfast at 8:00 a.m. by a lovely team of people with smiles on their faces. I must say the smiles on their faces were more comforting than the food they were serving. Once breakfast was finished, they would ask what we wanted for lunch, then the nurses would come around and give us bed baths, make the beds, and generally have a tidy/clean up. Twelve noon was lunch—I must say I was impressed with the choice offered, and the lunch menu was not that bad. I generally had a sandwich and soup. You can't go terribly wrong with them. Dinner was served at 5:00 p.m., and I used to live on their lasagna and all their fattening carbohydrate foods, just in order to build up some strength. By this time, I had lost over fourteen pounds in the hospital, and there was a need for me to consciously fatten up and get some exercise in.

Before my illness I was very fit and healthy. Emil and I would only eat brown foods, fresh fruit and vegetables, and not much fried food at all. I would go to the gym every day and swim 1 mile a day, three times a week. The other two days I would be in the weights section or on the running machines doing a 3.1 mile run. So, being sick and in bed all day was totally out of my comfort zone.

After every meal, I would make an effort to walk a couple of miles down the various corridors just to try and build up my strength and get my body back to as close to normal as possible. Also, I wanted to get my stoma working well, and walking is great for that. I would visit the children's ward or pass the operating theater toward various day clinics, and so on. I was not very adventurous, but it was all I could do to try and get some exercise in. There was also a pretty good Costa Coffee downstairs, so I would go down with Emil when he came to visit and indulge in my beloved coffee. I really missed my little double shot of coffee in the mornings at home. I found myself drinking tea in the hospital, which I never do. I have to admit, I am a bit of a coffee snob; for me, it is all or nothing.

To my mind, always being a very healthy person, eating the right foods and exercising daily, was part of my ethos. Being in hospital, lying down, and feeling sorry for myself was not an option. I know I pushed myself and my surgeon pushed me as well, and I am forever indebted to him for this. He was keen to get rid of my catheter as soon as possible, as well as my drainage bag and antibiotics. He was also keen for me to be discharged early and to be able to take care of myself.

Visiting hours at the Croydon University Hospital were between 2–5 p.m. and then 6–8 p.m. The nurses would do their rounds at 8:00 in the morning, 2:00 in the afternoon, and 8:00 and 11:00 at night. They would administer the tablets to everyone and check our vital stats. It was at this time that I realized it would be better for me to cut down on some of the tablets they were prescribing me. I managed to get rid of the antinauseant tablets and steroids, which made me feel a lot better. The only tablets I kept taking were Buscopan for my stomach pains. To my mind, the fewer tablets I took, the sooner my body would recover to as close to normal as possible. Also, I hated swallowing tablets.

The nurses, toward the end of my stay, would ask me for a briefing of the ward—it was a standing joke as I would try and help everyone in the ward if the nurses were busy. I remember one morning, little Iris had slipped out of her chair onto the floor; fortunately a nurse and I were able to grab her before she hit the floor. Iris was very distressed, and I think it was probably the memory of the nursing home accident when she fell out of bed. I had to shout at her to calm down—I did feel guilty afterwards, but she was getting quite distressed. She smiled afterwards and joked about it, so all was good.

To be brutally honest, a couple of mornings I would wake up and wonder who would look after me today. I was getting tired of not sleeping but also from looking after the ladies in the ward, taking them to the toilet, and so forth. I often used to pray that God would give me the strength to carry on and keep me smiling—and He did. I know that I had the Great Physician on my side, and He was by my side throughout, answering all my prayers, and looking after me; what more could I want!

One morning I woke up and decided I was going to treat the hospital as a holiday camp. Thinking about it while lying in bed, I thought what could be better: food brought to you at mealtimes, clean linen daily, nurses ready to help whenever—what could be better. That was the start of my mental change in mood, starting to relax and go with the flow.

Every other day I would get visits from the surgeon and his team and also from the stoma nurses. I also had a couple of physio sessions to help me walk and climb stairs. After a couple of sessions, they gave up on me as I was walking faster than they were. Everyone seemed extremely pleased with my progress and could not believe how agile I was—thank you Lord! When my surgeon came to see me, I used to call him "My Maker's Helper." He truly had a unique gift and knowledge given to him, and he was amazing. It was quite funny to hear how the surgeon used to say how beautiful my scar was looking, and when the stoma nurses came they used to say how beautiful the colostomy was looking—I would never have said beautiful. There was an elderly lady in the ward next door who had a very similar operation to mine, as well as a colostomy. I was told that she had been in the hospital recovering for nearly a month and would be discharged shortly. A whole month—not a chance—please, Lord!

On the Monday I got a visit from a couple of work colleagues in the hospital, it was great to see them, and get some normality back. I got sick in the middle of their visit, which was a bit embarrassing—but welcome to hospital wards. That Thursday, I got another visit from four work colleagues of mine, plus one of their babies. It was lovely to see them all traipsing through to my bed with a push-chair. Although the rules were only two visitors at a time, no one seemed to mind, and everyone loved to see baby Jonathan—he was a true blessing to all of us. Just hearing baby noises and holding him and talking nonsense was lovely. I forgot for a moment about hospital life.

The week went by so quickly with regular visits from colleagues, friends, and of course my sister every after-noon, and husband in the evenings. I also got a visit from the gynecologist who removed my one ovary—unfor-tunately she was getting into so much technical detail I fell asleep half-way through the conversation, without knowing it. Emil told me afterward what she said; I did feel really bad. I also received a couple of visits from the dietician at the hospital. I don't mean to be rude, but she was not a good advertisement for eating healthy as she was rather rotund. She was very sweet and told me that during my first six weeks at home, I was not to eat any-thing but white foods, such as white bread, white pasta, white cereals, and definitely no fruit and vegetables. I was horrified; I normally eat a lot of bran and brown foods, and of course a load of fruits and vegetables. I was surprised by this, but she said that my colostomy at this stage, and my system generally, could not handle any harsh foods. I was so not looking forward to my new change in diet, but it had to be done. Don't argue and just get on with it.

The Friday before I was discharged, I was scheduled for a CT scan in the morning. Of course, I was dreading going down as they would put a cannula in my arm, so they could inject me with iodine to see the contrast in the scan better. By this time I was looking like a pin cushion and was so sick of needles. Every other day, the phlebotomist would come in and take blood samples. I used to dread her coming in and trying to find a vein. This was despite all the other needle marks from the drips, and so on. I prayed the Lord would help the nurses find a vein easily—and they did, on the top of my hand. The CT scan was to see if the cancer had spread at all to my top part of my body. Or course I was very anxious about this, but the peace that God gave me while waiting for the results was amazing. I prayed that the Lord's will be done in my life. After all, my life is not my own; I belong to Him—what a comfort. God's will for our lives is to live abundant, fulfilled, healthy lives, and so I know only good things are on the horizon.

Saturday came around, and Emil visited me pretty much all afternoon and evening. We even went down to the coffee shop in the hospital lobby and had a very heartfelt, tearful conversation. I think I was probably at my lowest that evening. I was nervous about the CT results and also about being discharged the next day. I had the comfort of nurses twenty-four hours a day if anything should go wrong, and of course, I appreciated the very clean, clinical environment. It is amazing how you get used to an environment so quickly with all its routines and quirks. Of course, my darling husband was as loving and patient with me as ever, and I can never thank him enough for all his patience, love, and support he has shown me throughout. When you say your marriage vows so many years ago, and it says "in sickness and in health," you really don't expect it to happen so soon, but Emil has been amazing and I thank God for joining us together as one.

Emil tucked me in for the night before he went off home. No apologies; Emil has tucked me away and kissed me goodnight from day one of our marriage. I realize I am an old lady now, but I treasure every time he does this. He was busy straightening my bed linen for me and tucking it under the air mattress when all of a sudden I felt the bed starting to deflate. I guess he must have accidentally unhooked the valve to the air in the mattress, and I found myself vanishing into the bed frame. It was rather embarrassing having to call a nurse over to try and sort out my deflated bed, and me. There I am, legs in the air, bottom stuck on the hard base of the bed—not a pretty sight. I would hate to know what she was thinking. Needless to say, that was the last time Emil attempted tucking me in again in the hospital, ever.

Sunday morning came and I finally got the CT scan results—all clear. I was over the moon and rang Emil and my sister to let them know. Breakfast was served at 8:00, and then I went straight to the bathroom to get washed all on my own. I took so long that I was interrupted with a knock to say that my chariot (aka wheelchair) was waiting for me to take me down to the chapel. It was great to be in the house of the Lord and fellowshipping with other believers and breaking bread. After the service had finished, I was wheeled back to the ward and had a good, hearty meal. I must say, the hospital food was growing on me, and I came to enjoy the meals served. There was a large variety you could choose from the menu, which was a bonus. They also catered for the different ethnicities in the hospital, and I loved the curries. It was probably not good for me, but I can't resist a good "ruby."

After lunch a couple of nurses asked if they could see me change my stoma bag—uuuuggghh! The nurses had emptied many stoma bags before, but I had never seen the bag being changed. I was more than happy to show them in the bathroom, and they were really excited about the whole thing. This is why I am not a nurse, and the nurses within the National Health Service deserve so much more than what they are getting. All kudos to them.

Sunday afternoon at 2:00, Emil came for visiting hours and also to pick me up and take me home. I was so happy and excited that I was doing cartwheels in my mind. We had to wait a while for the hospital discharge letter and, of course, a massive plastic bag full of medication, dressings, wipes, and so forth. The nurses were very thorough and had also arranged for a district nurse to come the following Friday to remove my staples in my tummy and for the stoma nurses to come to my house for regular home visits.

We finally left my sanctuary at around 3:30 on Sunday afternoon, where a taxi was waiting to take us home. It was such a happy but scary moment, not knowing what the future would be like without all the nurses around. Thank God for Emil and Jessica; I can never repay them for all their sacrifices made for me. I only ended up staying in the hospital for ten days—I cannot believe how fast and trouble-free my recovery was, and I thank the Lord Jesus Christ for this.

When I left the hospital I was weighing 106lbs, which was light for me. In the ten days, I had lost over a stone in weight. The nurses would weigh each patient every day on this chair with a scale attached to it. It reminded me of baby wards, I suppose. In a very warped way, I quite enjoyed getting back to my old weight from twenty years earlier, but I looked like a bag of bones, I have to admit. My posture was not very good, either, what with the scar running from my pubic bone all the way above my navel and also the stoma bag; I looked an old hunched back lady. I had to start concentrating on putting on weight and improving my posture. I knew that once I got home I would be fattened up in no time—we love our food and eat vast quantities of healthy food. We have a good diet but eat far too much—but then again life is short, so why not!

I have also cut my coffee consumption massively. I now only drink one cup of coffee a day, instead of ten. I find I am drinking a lot more fruit juice and water, which is not a bad thing.

I cannot stress enough to other cancer patients how important it is to start exercising and eating as soon as you possibly can after an operation. Try to get your routine in life back as soon as you possibly can. The worst thing you can do is to wallow in self-pity and play the victim. You have to imagine yourself well. God gave us an imagination; let us use it for good things and to see ourselves whole and well.

Some days I have not felt like doing anything, but I have consciously not stayed in bed at all and sat in a chair and got my own dinner and done my own laundry. I have vacuumed and dusted and done all the mundane housework, but housework has been a great form of exercise. It is very easy to get complacent about your recovery and expect things to be done for you, but that is not a clever way to move forward and start healing from the inside out. You need to push yourself every day to get the energy and move.

Chapter Five

Life at Home

J must just mention as background, that in February, 2013, Emil and I were talking about downsizing. We had moved into our family home ten years prior, and virtually overhauled the house with a huge addition, conservatory, back garden, and so on. We poured a lot of blood, sweat, and tears doing the house up and enjoyed the fruit of our labors for the ten years we were in the house. However, with no kids (not out of choice), it was time to sell the big family home. Emil loved the house more than I did in a way, probably because I had to clean four bathrooms and five bedrooms. We worked out that Emil was in charge of the outside of the house and the inside was mine, although Emil was in charge of the kitchen. To be honest, Emil is a better cook than I am, but I do all the baking. Emil would spend most weekends in the garden, tidying up, picking up leaves, weeding, and doing all the work entailed in keeping a tidy garden. We missed spending time together on weekends, so it was time the house went to a family.

We went out of curiosity and coaxing to see a new development of apartments in our local area; needless to say we fell in love with the apartment and virtually offered on the spot. Back in February, 2013, nobody could predict what the housing market was going to do, so we put in a cheeky offer and thank the Lord, it was accepted. The apartment was not on sale at all, but it was the only one we were interested in, and our offer was accepted. We exchanged contracts in March and duly put our house on the market. To get Emil to agree to sell the house was a huge feat in itself, but the Lord knew what lay ahead, and that the house would be too much for me later on. What a loving, caring, thoughtful God we serve, that he should be interested in our small insignificant lives to such a degree as finding us the perfect place to recoup and live in for years to come.

We finally sold the house in September, 2013, just before the cold weather set in. We rented a two-bedroom apartment in the same complex as our new apartment, as ours would not be complete until June or July of 2014. The flat we rented was a lot easier to keep clean, and it was a whole lot warmer than the house would have been. So, God works behind the scenes and knows the beginning from the end in each and every one's lives. The flat was a perfect place to recoup in and concentrate on healing and wholeness. Thank you, Lord!

Life seemed to get a routine pretty quickly when I returned home, which was good. I like routine, and am generally a little bit OCD on time-keeping and tidiness. There is nothing worse than people being late for appointments when they have agreed a set time; unfortunately that includes hospital appointments—that is my rant for the book!

Jessica stayed with us for the first month of my recovery, and I don't know how I would have gotten through the days without her help and support. Emil used to leave the house at 6:00 a.m. for gym and work every day, and I would pretty much be up by then for the day. In my mind, I wanted to try and stick to a time routine that I was used to. I was always thinking at that time of my returning to work and not falling into laziness, but keeping up the regular time keeping I have done for twenty-plus years.

Jessica would come into my room at 8:00 with my beloved double shot of coffee for the day—it was like nectar to me. She would then wash me around 10:00, and I have to say, I have never felt so vulnerable in all my life. I am usually so independent, so for someone to do everything for me is very disconcerting. When we washed, we had to be very careful that the dressings over the staples did not get wet, so I would have to kneel in the bath holding onto the sides while we washed my back, which was very odd but it worked. I did so miss my long soaks in the bath and all the bubbles; those were the good old days. When Jessica left on the weekends then I was wholly reliant on Emil for washing, feeding, and clothing me. I would then go downstairs into our conservatory and sit overlooking the garden for pretty much most of the morning. We would then walk around the neighborhood in the afternoon and have a late lunch. It was a lovely, hot summer and just reading and listening to music and chatting was very sweet. Nearly every other day, I would have visitors in the house; whether work colleagues, friends or nurses, there was always someone around, which was really nice. My friends used to arrange it that if Jessica wasn't around, someone would be at home with me, and I was very touched by them all for their thoughtfulness.

The Wednesday I got back from the hospital, I had the stoma nurses visit me, and by this time I was proficient in changing and cleaning the dreaded stoma bag. I hate to get into too much detail but even to this day I still gag at changing my bag. In my mind this is just not normal, and I hated seeing this thing stuck on my body. I know some people live all their lives with a colostomy, but for me this was worse than cancer! I suppose it is because I am relatively young and fit and liked going swimming in the gym every morning and taking a sauna afterward or going to do weights in my Lycra trousers. It is something I have had to get used to, and it does help that I lived in my baggy pajamas most days, so no one can see when my bag is full of gas. As Jessica used to joke, "I always knew she was full of hot air." Jessica also wanted me to name my stoma—I was totally not happy to do this. She named it Susan but to this day it irritates me—this is something that is not right and normal and it is just a thing stuck on my body until I get the reversal—period.

On the Friday I had the district nurse come around in the morning to remove my staples in my tummy. The stitches looked like a big silver zipper, not too dissimilar to a jeans zipper. I was so nervous and to be honest, sweating buckets while she was doing it. There were fifteen steel staples from my pubic bone to just above my navel. The surgeons were very thoughtful and actually cut around my navel so I still have it. I have got to admit; my scar does look beautiful. Emil said next time we go on holiday I should stand next to some people with tattoos and say that "girls have tattoos; look at my scar!" Jessica has a scar on her tummy which runs horizontal, while my scar is vertical—so we would be a picture. In fact, we were joking that we should do a tattoo of a zip for both of us and have butterflies and flowers coming out saying "all things bright and beautiful." Don't worry, we were only joking. I don't get why people would tattoo themselves or go through cosmetic surgery unnecessarily. Save it, God forbid, for when you really need needles, and so forth.

While the nurse was removing the staples, Jessica was holding my hand. I have got to say that Jessica is not the best person with a good constitution when it comes to blood and gore. During the whole episode, she was looking outside the window and telling me how great the scar looks and how easy the staples are coming out, but unless my sister has eyes in the back of her head, she was telling a good lie. I do appreciate Jessica for being with me through all the sicknesses and needles; this is definitely not her comfort zone. After all her radiotherapy sessions and her cancer, I don't blame her. Just the smell of hospitals is very unsettling to both of us now.

Chapter Six

Chemotherapy

$\mathcal{B}$efore I started with my chemotherapy, I was asked to see the team of cancer specialists at the Royal Marsden in Sutton. When I first met them, it was amazing to see how young they were and how very knowledgeable. They mentioned that I had Stage 4 cancer, and as a result they would be giving me aggressive chemo, as I was young and could handle it. It was decided to give me nine cycles of chemo every fourth week. I would have a consultation the first day, I would get an IV administered on the second day, and two weeks of tablets thereafter. The third week, I would be free of any toxins, and then on the following Monday the cycle would start all over again.

Jessica went with me for the initial consultation, and when they saw us together they could not believe how similar we looked. When we explained we were actually identical triplets, they decided to do genetics testing on me as well, which was great, as my nieces and nephews would benefit from this. They heard that Jessica had breast cancer a few years earlier and that my father passed away from cancer of the kidney, as well, twenty years earlier.

They also ran through my operation procedure and mentioned they were performing histology on my tumor. This meant that they were still unsure if the ovary they removed, which was full of tumors, spread to the colon via blood or contact. They were looking at the nine centimeter tumor they took out of my colon and would let me know the results at a later stage. All this was fascinating, but to me, personally, the less I knew about things the better.

I was then asked to see the chief clinician administrator who ran through the various procedures and what I should expect from chemo. When I saw the long list of side effects I should expect, such as diarrhea, nausea, mouth ulcers, and even the worst case, death, I just prayed that the Lord would carry me through my journey and that his love and strength and joy would enfold me. I knew it was not going to be an easy ride, and that I was totally reliant on the Lord to get me through. I am such a coward, especially after the hospital stay which was full of needles. Being a chemo patient, there is no way you can even worry about needles; these are the least of your worries, and I soon found that out.

I was then asked to do a CT scan so that they could take scans before chemo started, during chemo, and after chemo so they could do comparisons. Of course this entailed being injected with iodine so they could see things clearer, and thank the Lord everything seemed clear on the scan.

On September 2 and 3, 2013, I finally started chemotherapy. In a way, I am grateful that I did not know quite what it entailed. I have so much admiration and sympathy for those cancer sufferers going through chemotherapy. I don't think anyone can truly understand the ordeal they go through or how much it takes out of them mentally and physically. You are literally on a roller-coaster ride where one day you feel fine, and the next day you literally cannot get out of bed. The first week is normally the worst, and then it gets better before you have to start the cycle all over again.

When I went for my first chemo session at the Royal Marsden, it was interesting and upsetting to see how many cancer patients there were, and of course, the young children just broke my heart. You go to the MDU (Medical Day Unit) and get allocated a zone and a chair number for the duration of your IV. You go to your seat, and a nurse will come and run through the procedure with you. All the nurses are very thorough and very sympathetic, and I am very grateful to them for all their help.

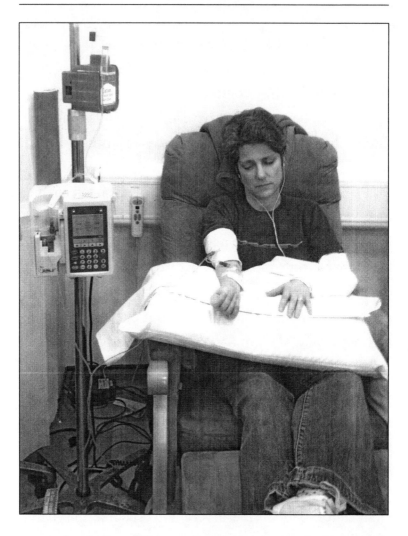

First of all, with the nurse inserts a cannula as there are a number of injections and fluids that need to be administered during the session through it. They also provide you with a warm electric arm blanket so you can wrap the arm that is going to take the IV. This helps alleviate any pain and stinging during the process. The first injection is a flush to clear the drain, and then you are given an antinausea injection. This is then followed by a steroid injection before the actual chemo is administered. Once your chemo session is complete, you are then given another ten-minute flush to clear the cannula tube.

Invariably, I would need to use the restroom during the IV. Trust me, two hours of sitting is a very long time for my constitution. It was a delicate maneuver, trying to get out of the armchair with your IV attached. You then had to get to the ladies' room, lock the door, and undress without disturbing the IV you have dragged along with you. I would try and remember to wear baggy, warm clothes with me so it was manageable. It was almost a whole aerobic exercise trying to "pay a penny."

Jessica was with me for the first four chemo sessions, and she was amazing. The hours she spent sitting next to me, reading and listening to music, could not have been easy. After the chemo session, we got home, and I went straight to bed. To be honest, not having had chemo before, I really did not know what to expect. I got the most incredible intense headache right in the middle of my forehead. You are also warned about tingling sensations in your fingers and toes; they were right. Also, just drinking any liquid is a pain for the first three days; you feel a choking sensation around your neck, which is very unnerving. Where they injected the toxins in my arm felt hard as a rock for a couple of days and was very sensitive so that even a bed sheet over my arm was painful.

Besides the above symptoms, I thank the Lord that I had not lost my appetite or hair. They had prescribed my chemo tablets for the two weeks, but they also had prescribed for me for the first three days steroids and anti-nausea tablets. I took all these tablets but found that the steroids were seriously making me pig out. It wasn't a bad thing after losing so much weight, but I knew it could not go on forever. I had food on my brain 24/7. Not a lot of cancer patients can say that, but I was eating so much food, it was embarrassing.

September 23 and 24, 2013, was my second chemo session. I kind of knew what to expect and just prayed beforehand that the Lord would help me get through this with a smile on my dial. Not a lot of patients at the hospital have smiles on their faces, and to me it was important to shine with the love of Jesus on my face. Jessica and I would often minister and talk to various patients who were on their own and just comfort them and tell them we were praying for them. Not once were we ever shut down or told to go away. You find, in circumstances like this, people are more willing and accepting of the Good Shepherd.

After the second session, we were on our way out, and I looked like a Michelin tire advertisement, all wrapped up. One of the nurses came running from the pharmaceutical office with a massive pink bottle of liquid. She gave it to me and said that I need to ensure that I wash my hair and body with this medical soap for the next five days. If anyone knows what I am talking about, this soap is what surgeons use in the operating room, as well as the nurses on the ward. It leaves your hair feeling like a damp mat without much of a smell. Apparently, I was carrying a mild form of MRSA, and I needed to adhere to this regime, which I did. When you first get into the MDU for your IV, they ask you to swab your nose, and this is how they found out I was carrying this bug. So, those tests do work, and I was very impressed but not amused!

October 14 and 15, 2013, was my third chemo session. I must say that my first three sessions went off relatively uneventfully. After my first session, I decided to stop taking the steroid tablets and antinausea tablets and only take the chemo tablets. The steroids were making me hairy and fat, and I just wanted to take the bare necessities required. I just trusted in the Lord to help me through the mild nausea and fight any side effects to His glory.

Emil and I moved to the rental flat on October 12 with the help of Jessica and her husband, Nick. October was a very busy month, packing boxes to go to storage, arranging moving men, finalizing the rental accommodations, and so forth. Looking back, it was a lot to take on, but it took my mind off my health and onto more pressing issues, which helped. I have always treated this cancer as an inconvenience. There were always more important things to sort out on a daily basis than this curse of cancer, and thank God for his mercies through it all.

On November 4, 2013, I went for my MDU appointment and blood test. I was quite surprised and also upset when I was told that the blood platelets in my bone marrow were too low for the IV to be administered the following day. Who would have thought that I would be desperate for the IV, but I was. I just wanted to get my sessions done and over with so I could move on with my "normal, boring life." As a result, the doctors delayed my treatment for a week.

It was once we moved, that I decided to get my act together and start exercising. There was a gym downstairs in the new complex, and I decided to use the running machines. Don't worry; I did not run. I just walked 3.1 miles each time I went. I must say that most of the time I went, I did not want to do the exercise but was glad afterward in what I had achieved. I was told by my surgeon that I would be unable to do any core/stomach exercises for a good couple of years from start to finish, but he encouraged walking. My main concern now is to not look like a "lollipop lady," with skinny legs and a big tummy.

Because my blood platelets were low the previous week, I got it in my mind to start eating liver. Don't ask me why, but I just thought liver would help. Poor Emil was coerced into eating loads of various liver salads and pates for the week. My favorite recipe, if anyone is interested, is lamb's liver rubbed in flour and paprika and fried in shallow oil. Then brown pitta bread stuffed with Greek yogurt, fresh mint, and the lamb liver—lovely jubbly. Maybe even a glass of Chianti; okay, I have been watching too many movies.

On November 11, 2013, I went back to see the MDU doctor and was told again that my blood platelets were too low to administer the IV. At that point, I was very upset and frustrated as I was feeling remarkably well. I mentioned that I was eating super healthy and had been doing gym three times a week, walking 3.1 miles each day in the third week. The doctor mentioned that it had nothing to do with fitness or diet; there was nothing I could do about it. He did, however, mention to enjoy another week off tablets, which I did.

On November 18, 2013, I went again for my MDU appointment and blood test. I was so relieved and happy to hear that my blood platelets were normal and was able to do IV on the nineteenth. Who would have thought that someone could be so excited about being given an IV! However, there is always a caveat to good news. I was told that instead of the normal two-hour IV session, they would be moving it up to a four-hour IV session, and lowering the toxicity in the tablets. So instead of five massive bomb-like tablets every day, I would get three massive bomb-like tablets and two smaller ones. To be honest, I was more than happy with that because I was finding swallowing so many big tablets a struggle. The other thing about those tablets is that they are so toxic, you are not allowed to touch them with your bare hands, and the instantaneous headaches you get after swallowing them is amazing. No, I did not wear gloves handling the tablets; I maneuvered them out the package and straight into the mouth. It was not very ladylike, but it did the job.

How the doctors have to weigh all the various conditions in each individual's body to determine dosage is quite special, and we are truly blessed in this country to be given such amazing treatment on the National Health Service. I know that in various other countries around the world, chemo tablets are astronomically highly priced, and I am very grateful for living in this country. I have never had the opportunity to need the NHS in the twenty-two years I have lived here, but they have excelled my preconceptions—despite the various negative news reports. I know that sometimes people are misdiagnosed and sent home too early, but there are thousands more who are alive today because of the care given by the NHS.

On December 9, 2013, I went back for another MDU appointment and blood test. The doctor I see is from Aleppo in Syria and a lovely man, very caring and thorough. The first thing I asked was whether I could do the IV session on December 10. He, of course, kept me in suspense and said he needed to run through a few things before he tells me. He mentioned that since lowering my tablet dosage, my blood platelets were fine—what a relief. He did, however, mention that my liver enzymes were low and that they would need to keep an eye on that.

On December 10, 2013, Emil and I arrived at the hospital at 9:30 a.m. for the IV. By this time, Jessica had found a job and was unable to come with me, so it was Emil's turn to pay his dues—poor man. Unfortunately, I had to have another four-hour session of IV, so I made sure Emil brought plenty of reading material with him. It was 3:15 p.m. by the time we left the hospital. After a four-hour session, you definitely get a numb bum, and it is a relief to walk afterward. However, now that the cold was settling in, I was finding the cold extremely painful. Just holding a glass or inhaling cold air was very uncomfortable. The biggest upset for me was that I could no longer indulge in my cold iced coffees anymore as it was far too painful to swallow. I can probably indulge in them on the third week.

On December 30, 2013, Emil and I attended another MDU appointment and blood test. We arrived at the hospital early so I went to the restroom. It's a good thing I did because, of all the things to happen, my colostomy bag had exploded. I could not believe it. I went to the customer care desk and asked if they could provide me with a colostomy bag. You would not believe the hassle it was to try and find one in a hospital! Finally one was sourced, and I could proceed onto the lab for my bloodwork. I was so conscious of smelling bad and being "Billy no Mates" (in the UK it means rejected and on your own) that I could not wait to get home and have a shower and forget about the whole sorry story. The good news at least was that I could do IV the following day, which was New Year's Day.

Jessica and Nick arrived early morning on December 31, and we proceeded to the hospital. I had baked the ward nurses a cake for New Year's, and we all were in good spirits, laughing and joking. It was great to have Jessica back with me at the hospital with her positive attitude and beaming smile. The nurse came to inject the cannula into my arm and unfortunately failed to find a vein on the first attempt—not good. I was sweating buckets by this time as I absolutely hate needles. My brother-in-law, Nick, mentioned that I should treat the needle as my friend. At first we did not get it, but then we all burst into laughter. Especially after he told the nurse he was happy to find my vein as he was quite good at it.

Nick used to be a drug addict for twenty years, imprisoned in four different countries (hence his fluency in Spanish and Dutch), and well known to the UK police. In other words, he had been a very bad boy. One day he was in prison in the UK when he picked up a Gideon Bible and started reading it and asked the Lord into his life. From that day on, he has not used drugs, and his life has turned 360 degrees. He now preaches in various prisons around the world and is a church leader, on fire for the Lord. I am just in awe of how God's grace can change, transform, and heal people from the inside out. No matter what people's pasts are, God loves them and draws them to Him, irrespective of persons.

After spending a good six hours in the hospital, we left to enjoy the festivities. Emil had cooked a lovely meal: Jessica's favorite (chicken in yogurt with fresh coriander and chili), and we spent the evening in front of the TV watching some movies. Unfortunately, I did not make it to midnight, so over breakfast we all wished everyone else God's blessings for the New Year. Nick and Jessica then left after breakfast to go back to exotic Essex.

On Friday, January 3, 2014, I woke up feeling absolutely awful. I could not get out of bed or even move; I was so lethargic. I know the doctors and nurses had warned me that as the chemo sessions went on for some time, the worse I will feel and the longer it would take me to recover from the IV. I had three more sessions to go, and I was trusting the Lord that I was going to feel better and stronger as I progressed. I had no doubt that He was in control and I needed to focus on Him and not my circumstances.

On January 20, 2014, Emil and I attended another MDU appointment and blood test. The nurse in bloods was a *big* lady; I have nothing against big people, but she was not too gentle and it was painful. When I got home that afternoon, my arm, where she took blood, was black and blue—not a very fetching color. The doctor mentioned that my blood platelets were low again, but fortunately they would do the IV the next day. They will just infuse me with 20 percent less toxins than previous. Unfortunately, it would still be the dreaded four hours, although he did ask if I wanted to do six hours so the chemo would go in slower. Thanks, but no thanks, was the appropriate answer to that, I believe. There is nothing worse than sitting in one spot for such a long duration with a needle in you, and it is painful. The doctor also mentioned that because I was still experiencing pins and needles in my fingers and toes for the full duration of the three-week cycle, they are considering not doing the eighth and ninth cycles of IV—just tablets.

I did mention that I would rather have long-term side effects than, God forbid, the cancer coming back. What was most interesting was that the doctor mentioned that the IV actually only accounted for 3 percent of the actual chemo; the tablets were more important. To be honest, I would just let the doctors and the Lord decides what is best. As for me, I would lay back and think good things and love all the people running after me, "milking it." The doctor delayed my cycle by one week, and Emil and I would see him next on February 17, due to my blood platelets being low—uuugghhh!

On January 21, I went for the dreaded IV. Who should be in the MDU but the same big nurse who took my blood the previous day? I was very tactful about it, and once she saw my arm, she understood; it was badly bruised. I asked if one of the senior nurses could install the cannula into my forearm, and she fortunately obliged. I must say I do love a bit of drama in my life, and it was certainly an interesting visit. After the IV had completed, I was suffering from intense chest pains and side pains. The nurses wheeled in the ECG monitor and started sticking stickers all over me; for one moment I thought someone was going to start throwing darts or something. They gave me a tablet to put under my tongue to dissolve and after fifteen minutes, released me to my warm, comfortable flat.

On February 17, we went back to our beloved Royal Marsden for bloods and to see the MDU doctor. The doctor had fantastic news and said that they would not be giving me an IV the next day. I was so relieved; I dreaded them trying to find veins and sticking in needles. However, I had to continue to take the chemo tablets for two weeks. I thought I could manage that. They also decided not to give me my ninth and final cycle of chemo due to the long-lasting side effects. I was so happy I could have cried. So basically, all I needed to do is pick up the tablets, and finish the final two weeks of this horrid episode in my life. Thank you Lord!

Throughout chemotherapy, I had been going to the gym in the third week, when there was no medication to be taken. I used to go three times a week, walking 3.1 miles every time. I also did some stretching and leg work on the mat, but very gently. I cannot wait for the day when I can do a massive cat stretch and really stretch out and lengthen my body. I have not been able to have a proper stretch since all this nonsense began.

I have to say that being able to eat well and exercise had definitely boosted my morale and made my body resilient to any negative bugs that may have been flying around. On chemo, you have no immune system whatsoever, so it is vital that you keep yourself away from the public as much as possible. To be honest, I had been going to church every Sunday up in London on the public transport and grocery shopping in supermarkets, and every time I walked into a crowded room I just pled the blood of Jesus over me and my body. Thank God, I had not picked up any germs while I had been going through chemo.

Chapter Seven

Life after Chemotherapy

*D*uring the week of February, I received four different letters in the mail from the Croydon and Marsden hospitals. One was to come in for an ultrasound, the other MRI and CT scans and also a colonoscopy—uuuggghhhh! I am just very grateful to the doctors for being so thorough and wanting to cross their t's and dot their i's. I am trusting the Lord that all is clear, and we can move on to the next stage which is the stoma reversal—I can't wait!

I know the doctors initially mentioned that I will need to wait a couple of months before the reversal as they want to get all the chemo toxins out of my body first. God willing, I am hoping to go back to work on April 1 and work solid for a couple of months before having the operation and recovering for a few weeks after. I know it sounds silly, but I want to get back to work before my colleagues forget who I am and they find a better replacement for me. Also, I want to get some normalcy back in my life.

Emil and I went to see Dr. Husada, my surgeon at Croydon University Hospital. He is a very nice, young, dynamic doctor who initially operated on me. The disappointing news is that he will be leaving the hospital to move on before my stoma reversal operation, and I will have to go to another surgeon. I was hoping to try and keep the consistency with surgeons as he was the one who knows all about me. However, my Father in heaven knows me best, and after all, He is the great physician who even knows how many hairs are on my head. So I am leaving it to the man upstairs to find me the right surgeon and get my body back to as close as possible, as close to normal as possible.

One of the letters that came in the mail was for me to do a colonoscopy/endoscopy. I have heard so many stories about how horrible the preparation drink is for this, so I was definitely not looking forward to drinking "wallpaper paste." One thing I can assure everyone is that it is not as dreadful as people say it is—honest. Forty-eight hours before the procedure you need to basically eat white foods, such as white rice, white bread, butter, and pasta. You must not eat any whole grains, fruit, or vegetables. Also, you may have no milk in your coffee or tea, which was hard. Twenty-four hours before the procedure you are not too eat but only drink the Moviprep laxative they give you to clear out your bowels. You have to drink one and one-half liters of water with the Moviprep in the morning and the same in the evening. Wow—it definitely works and you need to make sure you are near a toilet. For those wanting to lose weight and feel nice and empty before putting on your little black dress—it works great.

Saturday, March 8, finally came around, and Emil and I went to the Croydon University Hospital for the procedure. The nurse who was going to look after me had such an amazing smile on her face and a shine that only children of God have. I asked her if she was a Christian, and of course she was. We were just talking forever about how great God is and such amazing love He has for his children. Also, that He is with us, whatever we are going through, and He never gives us more than we can handle. Amen!

We prayed together, and then I was wheeled into the operating theater. It did bring back some flashbacks about my operation in July last year but the doctor and nurses in the theater were more relaxed, and they do this procedure all the time. I was given two gowns to put on; one had to be front to back and the other back to front. This was due to them going into my colostomy as well as my "jacksie" (that is what Jamie Oliver calls it!) Also, before being wheeled into the theater I was given a really sexy pair of *big* pants—a lot bigger than Bridget Jones I might add. Silly me, they had an opening in the front and I took it for granted that they gave me the wrong pants, and that these were for men, so I put the opening to the front desperately trying to cover the opening with the elastic. I was also trying to make a fashion statement secretly—not. Anyway, once in theater, I was told that the pants I put on were back to front! At this stage I just wanted the procedure to be over with and save my blushes. So, with my big mouth I told the doctor and nurses that once I am under they can do what they like as I have left my dignity at the door a long time ago. I have never had this procedure before so I will know for next time. I have been told that I will need to have a colonoscopy/endoscopy once a year for the first five years after surgery—can't wait!

I also started telling the doctor that I had just finished my chemo tablets that week before he stuck me with the anesthetic. I later had nightmares of me going down from the anesthetic with my mouth open half way through my sentence, dribbling all over the floor—not a pleasant dream.

I woke up forty-five minutes later in the ward with the pants turned the other way around—I do not want to know how they did it, but full kudos to them. I then got dressed, and Emil took me home. I can vaguely remember how I got home and went to bed to sleep it off. The moral of the story is: (1) Moviprep is not that bad; (2) put your pants with the opening to the backside; and (3) wear that little black dress soon, before you start eating again.

On March 11, I had to go to Royal Marsden for an ultra-sound. It is very interesting to see your insides on screen, although the jelly was a bit cold. I was not too sure why I needed the scan but was told that they were looking at the liver as they were slightly concerned about it once the chemo tablets had finished. I was told that it looked normal although a bit coarse on the outside due to the chemo tablets. Well, in the scheme of things at least it is coarse inside and not outside. Due to the chemo tablets I have noticed that my skin breaks out a bit and with the steroids being pumped with the IV, I have gotten a little bit more hairy—very fetching.

Monday, March 17, we had an appointment to return to Royal Marsden to see one of the team members to run through a few things. First of all, I had to go to the lab and provide them with a blood sample. While I was sitting in the chair waiting my turn, I was just thanking the Lord for his daily mercies and that the end is near. After a seventy-minute wait to see a member of the team, I was told that I had the all clear. They did mention that I would need to come back in August for a CT scan. This would be done annually for the next three years so they can map out the scan to see any abnormalities, if any. They also mentioned that I was at high risk due to the tumor on my ovaries which had then transferred into my colon. There was a 50 percent chance of the colorectal cancer recurring. Also, they told me that one in three people develop cancer, which is a phenomenally high percentage and I was shocked to hear that statistic.

The doctor asked me to go back to the lab and give another blood sample as he would like to see the liver status. Okay, so the Lord has a sense of humor as He knows how much I sweat like a pig and dread needles, even after all this time and treatment. I must say I was not happy to get another needle in my other arm on the same day, but it had to be done—so stop moaning and deal with it. I always pray beforehand that I won't feel anything, and they get the sample first time. It seems to be working; thank you, Jesus.

As a treat, after five hours at the hospital, we finally caught the bus back to Sutton and had a lovely pig-out meal at Nandos. I had the most intense headache you could imagine. I think it was just from waiting around and also seeing some desperately sad sights at the hospital. Let me tell you, no matter how bad you are feeling yourself, even if you don't want to do anything, not even to get out of bed, remember, there is someone worse off than yourself somewhere in the world.

On March 24, while relaxing in bed over breakfast I received a telephone call from a team member at Royal Marsden to say that instead of waiting until August for the CT scan, they would like to do one as soon as possible. I must say, whenever the phone rings, my heart jumps a bit wondering who it could be. Apparently, my tumor markers internally are up, and they need to see what is going on. I did mention to the doctor that I was planning to go back to work on April 1, so if they could do the CT at their earliest, that would be most helpful. I had a knot in my tummy when the doctor put the phone down. I dreaded to think what lay ahead as I was getting very tired of this emotional rollercoaster I was on. One minute you have the all clear, and the next, your tumor markers are up.

Half an hour later, I received a call from the CT Department to say that I could come in tomorrow for the scan—thank you Lord. I just want to do as many appointments as possible before going back to work fulltime without any disruptions to my work life. That being said, I received a letter in the post last night to say that I have an appointment with the new surgeon who is taking over Dr. Husada's patients. Unfortunately, the appointment is at the Purley War Memorial Hospital and not Croydon University Hospital, and it is scheduled for May 22, 2014. I trust the Lord that this meeting is to discuss my stoma reversal, hopefully in June. The sooner the better.

Well, to be honest, March 24 did not start off very well with the news. The uncertainty of not knowing why the tumor markers were up, and what it meant going forward. I found myself on my knees in the middle of the room crying and praying all at the same time. Sometimes, emotions took the better of me, and I found myself in uncontrollable tears. My faith throughout this ordeal had been tested to its utmost, but I had no doubt that what the Lord Jesus has in store for me is only good.

When you get a phone call like the one I had this morning you automatically think of the worst case scenario—I guess that is only human nature. I prayed that I might have the strength to go through whatever is thrown at me. Please Jesus, no more chemo. These days, I don't seem to know what to pray anymore; I am at a loss for words. I am so conscious that the Lord knows the desires of my heart beforehand, and that whatever I pray He knows already. I thank God that I have this time to draw close to Him and that I have been given this unique opportunity to get right with Him, no matter the outcome. I feel desperately sorry and heartbroken for those souls who have died and not had an opportunity to draw close to their Maker, Father, and Friend.

I look at myself as being in a unique position of being in a win-win situation. If the Lord takes me home, then I will be with Him for eternity rejoicing with the other saints. If I survive this horrible ordeal, then I will be able to spend more time with my beloved Emil, family, and friends.

I have a lot to live for right now, and I would love to see our dreams come to fruition. I have drawn up a bucket list of all the things I would like to see and do. Our new apartment will be complete in June or July, and I would love the opportunity to furnish it and live in it for a while. This illness has really awakened in me how short life really is and how someone can be here in your midst one day and be gone the next. Considering I was only given twenty-four hours to live back in July last year, I am so grateful I have survived this long.

I had been watching closely the demise of Flight MH370 and how desperately sad the whole situation was. Nobody at the time knew exactly what happened, but how those poor souls were planning on a five-hour plane trip to be reunited with their loved ones only to be lost at sea.

On March 26, Emil and I arrived at the first-floor CT Department at Royal Marsden. Needless to say I had another cannula put in my arm—uuuugggh (have I mentioned I hate needles). They took a few scans and injected me with iodine to see a better contrast within my body.

On Thursday, March 27, I went to the Croydon University Hospital to see the stoma nurses. What a lovely bunch of ladies they are. They have my full respect—I could not do what they do with a smile on my face. I mentioned that I had not received my biopsy results from the colonoscopy earlier in the month. Debbie was so sweet and looked up my notes on the system and it was a huge relief to see that the biopsy was all clear. I mentioned to her that the Marsden did a CT scan yesterday and that they were concerned about the tumor markers being high. She asked if I would keep them posted as to the results.

I did feel a little embarrassed as I started crying for no apparent reason while I was with Debbie. I apologized profusely, but I just find these days with the roller-coaster time I have been through, it happens more and more that I just cry—ridiculous. Sometimes I have to talk to myself and tell myself I must stop being a drama queen and deal with the situations as situations arise. I am also constantly on my knees, singing and praying and trusting Jesus that His will be done in my life and that things will happen quickly without any pain. I have on my mind that song: "I'm trading my sorrows, I'm trading my pain, I'm laying them down for the joy of the Lord." I know that the Lord's will in my life is to live long and strong and that He only wants what is best for me. Sometimes I am at a loss for words for how to pray, but know that I serve a good God who loves me unconditionally.

I went back home after visiting the stoma nurses to receive a call from the Royal Marsden to ask me to come in and see the team on Monday, March 31, in the afternoon. I know within myself, it is not a good indication that they want to see me that soon. Needless to say I put the phone down and immediately sang praises to the Lord, as well as cried. I found that the waiting game is not my forte. I am the most impatient patient a hospital could wish for. Funny enough, one of my work colleagues, before I went in for my last operation, did mention that I must try not to dictate to the doctors. To be honest, I would have preferred if someone tell me the news over the phone than wait all through the weekend to hear the results in person. I rang Emil straight away at work and asked if he could take Monday afternoon off and take me to the hospital—it is always good to go with someone for moral support, and the hospital encourages it as well.

Sunday, March 30, was our eighteenth wedding anniversary—neither Emil nor I were in the mood to celebrate, so we came home after church and Emil cooked a lovely meal for us.

On Monday, March 31, I got up with a slight heavy heart. I knew that this day had come, and we were finally going to hear what was wrong. I really found the waiting game a lot harder than the actual results. I felt desperately sorry for the elderly folk who have to wait for biopsy results. The appointment was in the afternoon, so I met Emil up in London Victoria train station and got some lovely sushi for the train trip to Belmont, just outside Sutton, where the Royal Marsden Hospital is located. After a forty-five-minute wait in the office, we finally got to see one of the team members.

She explained that I had a new tumor growing on my tummy wall which was pushing on my bladder, which explains a lot! The doctor was pretty positive that it was isolated and that I would need a PET scan very soon and thereafter discuss the way forward. This may involve radiotherapy or an operation, but that would be determined by the scan. For the moment we were standing on God's promises in his Word; of blessings not curses, and that I am healed by His stripes. He has paid the price for my healing 2,000 years ago.

So now we wait.

Chapter Eight

Just When You Think It Is All Over

$\mathcal{T}$uesday, April 1, I finally got back to work and see my lovely colleagues. I thought April Fool's Day was quite appropriate for my return back to work. Everyone seemed genuinely pleased to see me, which is always a lovely boost to my ego. The first couple of days I felt like a little doggy, going around the secretaries' desks marking my territory and workspace. Of course it is nothing like that, but just the thought made me smile.

The first morning I got into the London Bridge train station, I had a little bit of a moment where a tear or two was spilled. Okay, I don't know what the other thousands of passengers must have thought, but I was just amazed how great God is that he has given me this opportunity to be back to as normal a life as possible. My first week back was lovely, catching up with everyone and everything.

After the first week, it was as if I had never been away. I arrived at work by 8:00 a.m. and tried to leave at 5:00 p.m., slightly earlier than normal working hours, but I was just so proud that I could make the first week and not feel too bad. I also looked like a pregnant forty-six-year-old, grey-haired lady. Because of my colostomy which is sitting right where waistbands should be, I had to purchase a couple of new dresses which were loose fitting. The one fear I had was looking like a "lollipop lady," with skinny legs and a big tummy. Unfortunately I think I did reach that point. The other benefit by being back at work was of course, that I slept much better after a full day of work, and I got to feel like my old self. Of course, those days I did not run for trains anymore; I just waited for the next one. I am not too sure if it was my illness or my age, but at that moment in time, I didn't care, just as long as I could continue on the upward spiral with God's help.

I have to say, my tummy is not feeling too good; I don't know if it was self-consciousness because I knew there was a tumor there, or if I was genuinely not well. I had to be so careful not to drink too much water before getting on public transport to try to keep my stoma bag under control. Sometimes it is not that easy in a crowded train. A couple of times when it has "gone off," I pretended I did not hear anything and just continued reading my book. Those days I was also not walking very fast, and my posture left much to be desired. I was consciously trying to walk straighter and not think I look twenty years older, walking with a stoop. I walked from London Bridge to my offices every morning, and it took roughly twenty minutes, so instead of the gym I was walking to work with thousands of other commuters. Oh well, times changed and I had to stop wallowing in my self-pity. God was in control, and I was excited to see what he had in store for me.

Lydda, our cleaning lady at the office, is a born-again Christian. She is about seventy years old and from Spain with very broken English, but she has the joy of the Lord in her and is always smiling and her eyes light up. She is amazing, and God definitely inhabits this lady; she is a true example of God's love. We often talk, and she mentioned that she had a friend that had a tumor and she used to pray over this tumor every day and rebuke it in Jesus' name. One day she went to the toilet and out popped these black tumors from within and she knew she was healed. Wow, I know miracles happen every day, and I am claiming mine to God's glory.

My whole desire throughout this all has been that work colleagues, family, and friends come to know Jesus better and to love Him more. I do not want to go through what I have without being a witness for Jesus, and I know He is going to prove Himself to those around. He is not going to ever embarrass me by not performing His mighty healing in my life. I know God has started a work in my life and He has not finished yet—to your name be all glory, Jesus.

I am not ashamed of the Lord Jesus and am always very happy to shout his name to anyone who listens about how He has brought me through my darkest days and given me such peace and joy through all obstacles I have had to jump. I could not have gone through what I have without Him—I am a coward and hate needles and anything to do with hospitals, so thank you, God, for your love and mercies every day.

My father died from cancer many years ago, and I remember visiting him in hospital and seeing how frail and vulnerable he looked. Jessica, my sister, was in hospital as well with her cancer, but thank God, she is alive today. So, as you can see, I do not have fond memories of hospitals. The last time I was in the hospital was for the removal of tonsils with my sisters. All three of us lay in the same ward, and it was fun. We were, however, only six years old, and that was the last time I had ever been in hospital.

So the shock for me was when I did land in hospital last year, the nurses wanted to wash me, and, of course, invariably, my having accidents in bed, was highly embarrassing for me. Now, I leave my dignity at the door and whoever wants to wash me or have a look at anything can help themselves. Thank you, Lord, for making me not feel self-conscious anymore or embarrassed.

On Tuesday, April 8, Emil and I woke up and had a lovely breakfast in bed. It was a nice lazy morning with a cup of coffee and TV in bed. We then left for the hospital at 11:00 a.m. for my PET scan. I must say I discovered a whole new wing at Royal Marsden I did not know existed. Every time I go to the Marsden, I am in awe of the skill and variation of each department and how many there are. I am now probably working my way through each department, after all the tests I have been having. Also, what strikes me is the amount of young doctors around. I know I am getting a bit long in the tooth, but some of them look barely out of school but all so very clever. God has certainly blessed them with a good brain, and they are using them in a most rewarding way.

My second week of work was exhilarating and exhausting all at the same time. I still found myself amazed that I am finally back "in the real world." I missed the buzz of the city and my work colleagues but not the commute. Before all this happened, I used to get the 6:00 train into the city and go to the gym before work. This enabled me to get a seat on the train in relative quietness, although snoring from a couple of commuters was the norm. These days, I am getting the 7:30 train, and I find myself being packed in the train carriages like a tin of sardines. As the weather gets warmer, I think the body odor is going to become an issue—something to look forward to!

I received a call from my clinical nurse from the Royal Marsden earlier in the week to let me know that my PET scan data was all in and that the Croydon University

Hospital and the Royal Marsden Hospital would be sitting down for a team meeting on Tuesday morning to discuss my case. Therefore, thank goodness, my appointment on Monday at the Marsden had been cancelled, and a doctor would call me after the team meeting on Tuesday to let me know what the next steps would be in order to get rid of this annoying tumor. Now it is just a waiting game, but I am standing on the promises of God and trusting that my tumor is going to disintegrate or disappear miraculously— why not; all things are possible to my Maker.

On Tuesday, April 22, I received a call early in the morning from Ramani, my clinical nurse at Royal Marsden in Sutton. She said that they had the weekly meeting; I was discussed, and the surgeons attended—hooray! Basically, the doctors were not sure the exact state of the tumor, whether it was interfering with my bladder or not. She mentioned that she would be arranging an MRI scan of my pelvis sometime this week and that I would need to call my surgeon at Croydon Hospital to arrange a meeting with him next week. I rang the surgeon's office, and his secretary left him a message to say that I had called. A couple of hours later, the secretary called back to say that Dr. Abulafi could see me this afternoon; I could not believe it. Usually it takes weeks to get an appointment into any surgeon's office—I was thrilled that things were moving so swiftly.

I left the office and arrived at Croydon University Hospital outpatients department for a 3:30pm appointment. If anyone knows any outpatients surgeries at all, it is usually a very long wait. An hour later I got to see Dr. Abulafi, and he explained that he would be arranging a cystoscopy (camera in the bladder) to see if there was any interference at all. At the moment, no one was sure what the state of the tumor was or even how they would approach the operation. He mentioned that Royal Marsden would be arranging the MRI of the pelvis. Dr. Abulafi then prodded on my tummy to feel where the tumor was and how it felt. I must say it was one of the most painful things ever. He did mention that if the tumor was solid and isolated and in no way interfering with the bladder, then the operation would be a relatively simple one. If there was interference then the operation would be more complex and would need to be done at the Royal Marsden in Chelsea. I asked him if I could then have my stoma reversal at the same time as the operation if it was the simple one, which he agreed with. Now we know, as a family of God, what we directly need to pray for: no interference with the bladder and two for one on the operation side—please, Lord!

I went back to work on Wednesday, April 23, and received a call in the morning to say that the MRI scans had been booked for the next day at 8:45 a.m. I am amazed how efficient the NHS is once a problem is discovered and how fast everyone works together to resolve the various issues. I thought it was quite amusing yesterday that while I was sitting in outpatient waiting room, they brought my file into the room. I have never had any need to use the NHS or ever visit a hospital. I never had an NHS outpatient file, but now it is steadily growing at a rapid pace, something like my tumor!

On Thursday, April 24, I went in the early morning to Royal Marsden in Sutton for the MRI scan. After catching two buses and having to wait twenty-eight between the two, it is absolutely exhausting by the time you get to the hospital. So, lying in the MRI scanner for forty minutes, listening to jazz music was a welcome distraction. Although the scan was very loud during the process, it was somewhat bizarrely very relaxing. I then had to get my blood tested again; it was getting difficult to try and find a vein as they were still bruised by the chemo and hardly visible. After the tests, I went back to work and was able to run for the train from Sutton to London and was pleased to have made it by the skin of my teeth.

For the past week, one of my brothers from South Africa had been visiting us, and it has been great to spend some quality time with him. I managed to leave work early and was able to squeeze an hour with him before he left for the airport. I also had a letter delivered to the flat from the Royal Marsden providing me with dates when to come in to have chemo. This of course made me panic and start desperately praying that this was a mistake. I rang Ramani early Friday morning to inquire about the letter and chemo dates, and fortunately she was just covering all the bases, taking the initiative to book the chemo session in case I needed it. Whew, please Lord—no more chemo in Jesus' name. Ramani did, however, mention that the MRI scans would be discussed at the Chelsea Marsden weekly meeting on Monday, so now we have to play the waiting game. In the interim, I was still waiting for Dr. Abulafi to arrange the cystoscopy at Croydon University Hospital, and I would chase him on Monday if I didn't get anything in the mail over the weekend. I am just desperate now to get rid of this tumor, and I can then start walking and running. Amen!

On Tuesday, April 15, one of the doctors rang my office to say that the PET scan showed that the tumor was isolated, and nothing was growing outside of it. Thank you, Lord. The tumor was large and growing rapidly. The doctor said that unfortunately none of the surgeons came to the weekly meeting so my case was not discussed but that they attend every other week and they would discuss my case next week. I kind of went into panic mode, I have to admit. I asked questions about the state of the tumor and what if it grew and exploded or the pain got worse, what do I do. I know it is negative talk and totally not of God, but you automatically panic. I had truly believed I was over any more cancerous tumors and that I had finally got my life back. This is another test I would have to go through with God's help. I cannot do it alone.

On Thursday, April 17, I rang my clinical gastrointestinal (GI) cancer nurse at Royal Marsden to say that the pain in my tummy is getting worse. She reassured me that as long as I was not nauseous, my stoma was working, and I was eating fine, then things were fine. She did urge me to take paracetamol regularly if the pain was severe. Later on that day I received a call back from my clinical GI cancer nurse to say that she had spoken to a doctor on the team and that if I was in any pain that was intolerable, I should go to the emergency room at Croydon University Hospital during the Easter break, which was starting tomorrow. That was one place I planned to avoid by all costs. She also mentioned that the doctor said that I may have to go through more chemo in order to shrink the tumor before they would operate on it. I was naturally devastated by this news. She mentioned that they may give me the same chemo IV and drugs as the last time with new antibodies included.

Any chemo patient will agree that chemo therapy is the worst part of all the treatments you have to go through. I just could not believe I might have to go through it all over again—why, Lord? I was getting angry and frustrated with God and constantly asking Him, why me? I could hear Him say—why not? I totally believe that God is in control of this horrible disease in my body and just like the disciples on the boat, when the storms were raging and they were getting anxious and scared, God was sleeping because He had the whole situation under control. It is during our toughest times, when God seems so distant, that He is at work. I am reminded of the footprints poem—God, where are you—we wonder where God is when things go wrong? I know that He is with me in the worst times possible, carrying me, holding me, reassuring me, and giving me the strength to face each day with the joy He has instilled in me. I have the peace that passes all understanding at this uncertain time, and I am standing on His promises.

Needless to say, when I got home Thursday evening I burst into tears and was absolutely dumbfounded why I had to probably go through all of it all over again. Emil was devastated as well, but that evening we just hugged each other and prayed about the whole situation. Sometimes I find myself lost for words and unable to explain God's rationale—then again, a mere mortal like me, how dare I even think I can understand the Almighty Savior. My initial thought and concern was for my work colleagues and friends who do not know the Lord; what would they think that I have not been healed after I had believed and expressed out loud God's goodness. I voiced my concerns to my pastor last Sunday, and he was so right. He said that God is not going to shame me; keep believing in Him and know that He is able.

The three-day Easter bank holiday weekend was the next day, which was nice to know that I had a few days to digest the news before going back to work. Easter Friday, Emil and I went to church and had an amazing celebration service, for Jesus has risen and lives forevermore—Amen!

On Saturday I had most of my family over to our little rental flat for coffee and Easter cake before viewing our new flat, which is due for completion in June or July. My brother from South Africa was visiting again, which was lovely and good to see him. He has been through a lot of trials over the past three years, but God had been faithful and answered all his prayers. After the flat viewing, we all walked to a lovely Iranian restaurant and completely pigged out on amazing food. If people have not been to an Iranian/Persian restaurant, then they are sorely missing out on some incredible cuisine. I often joke and say that the reason why I married Emil was for his lovely, delicious cooking. Often when we have dinner parties, I am in charge of the appetizers and dessert. I must say I tend to do a lot of Persian mezze starters anyway. Emil is in charge of the main dishes, and he usually cooks a couple of Iranian stews and saffron rice, which is absolutely delicious.

We then all walked back to the flat after stopping off for some lovely gelato ice cream in town. Okay, so we managed to find a gap in our tummies for dessert. My family has been such a blessing and constantly hold me up in prayer. I was told that my sister in Australia and her husband, along with my sister and her husband in England, and my brother and his wife were all going to fast on Tuesday and pray for my healing. I am so incredibly blessed to have such a family of faithful brothers and sisters in the flesh and the Lord. I am also totally grateful to my parents for bringing me up in a Christian household and instilling in us the fundamentals of lifewith Jesus, the head of our lives.

Throughout the month of April, I had been working full time back at my lovely job in the city of London and enjoying every moment of being back. Of course it would happen that while I was back a dozen people's birthdays fell in the month so, of course, I had to bake! Every time it is someone's birthday in the office, I bake. It has become a kind of tradition, and everyone seems to enjoy it.

Everything seemed to be going so well until Thursday, May 1. I guess Satan was not happy seeing me rejoice in the Lord in all circumstances, and the evil one wanted to rock my boat. When he does that, of course, I won't lie; initially I get downhearted but then realize the circumstance I am in and I lean on Jesus and start praying and worshiping Him until the pain eases away and my joy is back. God is so good, and His love for me is everlasting, enduring, and unfailing.

Chapter Nine

Hospital Holiday Camp 2

*O*n Thursday, May 1, I had to leave work early as I was in a lot of pain, and Emil and I went to the emergency room in Croydon, arriving around 4:00 p.m. on a cold, wet, and miserable afternoon. I went up to the emergency room desk to register myself, but I could hardly walk or talk from the pain, so I left it to Emil to answer the questions and show them my cancer patient card. Basically, when you become a chemo patient, you get a yellow credit card-size piece of paper which explains to the emergency room that they need to see the patient within an hour and if need be, administer IV drugs. Fortunately this worked, and we got to see one of the emergency room nurses within the hour.

Of course, there had to be dreaded needles somewhere, and as soon as we had finished the consultation, she put a cannula in my arm and took me to one of the side rooms where there was a bed and the sexy hospital gowns I had to put on while waiting for a doctor. In the interim, another nurse came in and put me on a drip and administered some drugs into my system, including morphine. Unfortunately, I think she administered the drug too quickly, and this caused me to faint—very embarrassing. Emil and I waited for some time until a doctor arrived. I must say, she could have been the age of my daughter, very young but very clever, asking all the right questions. Of course, before she came in, she looked at my history on the system, and she admitted it took some time to read through all the notes. I had to chuckle to myself, thinking a year ago I had no NHS records as I had never been sick; now there is a whole encyclopedia of me. Another lovely emergency room nurse came in and administered more morphine but this time very slowly and by the end of my stint in the emergency room I had a total of 15 mg of the morphine (I think I mentioned earlier on that morphine is rat poison!). I found out that little piece of information last year while in hospital, but to be honest, anything to get rid of the pain is welcome in my body at this time.

Emil left me around 7:00 p.m. in the emergency room and went home to get changed into comfortable clothes and to get me an overnight bag once he heard that they were admitting me into a ward. I made sure he did not forget the essentials like my stoma kit and toothbrush. Emil finally got back around 8:30 p.m. with all the goodies in the bag, and we sat and chatted for an hour or so while I was under observation. To be honest, I don't remember much from my time in the emergency room, but that was probably just as well. I heard a lot of moaning from beds next door and even a domestic squabble going on—the things these poor hospital staff are put through I can only imagine.

Emil then left me around 10:30 p.m. just before they wheeled me up to the wards. When they told me that I was going to Queens 1, I was so excited and happy. That was the ward I was in last year for my duration of recovery, and all the nurses were amazing. We finally got to the ward and straight away recognized the three nurses on night duty—thank you, Lord. It was a bit embarrassing, however; they asked me to get out of the bed that the porters brought me in and walk to the bed in the ward I was going to stay in. The next minute I remember being picked up from the floor by the nurses and almost carried to the bed. I had fainted again. I think it was all the morphine that I was given, and of course I was violently ill twice that night and once the following morning. Besides morphine making me constipated as a side effect, it also makes me violently ill. Morphine at the time is amazing, but the side effects are not good.

However, there is always a light at the end of the tunnel. I had a window-view bed again—how awesome is that! I was literally in the same bed as last year, just in a different bay. Thank you, Lord, for your goodness and thoughtfulness. I love spending hours watching the sky outside change and listen to people on the street walk by, and God knew that (He gives the desires of your heart), so here I was again at a window bed. The other amazing thing I heard was that Dr. Abulafi, my surgeon/consultant, was the consultant on call at the hospital over the weekend. God is amazing; everything dovetails together perfectly in His time, not ours.

The next morning I got up early around 5:00 to call Emil and see if he was up for work, which he was. During my conversation with Emil over the phone, I had to cut him short as I was ill; fortunately, I had gone to the toilet to make the call so no one could hear our conversation. I love that time of morning in the ward when everyone is sleeping. The sun is just rising, and the world seems at peace.

After speaking to Emil and washing up, I went back to bed and read my Bible for a while until the ward started waking up. It was nice to meet the ladies on the ward and hear their stories; there were definitely some strong characters among them, and the mix of people was interesting, to say the least. One of the ladies was a recovering drug addict: a rough diamond with a heart of gold.

Friday passed very slowly for me, and I was constantly looking at my Blackberry and keeping abreast of work emails. My bum also became numb a couple of times from just sitting on it all day doing nothing. On Friday afternoon, I was carted down to x-ray unexpectedly to have full frontal x-rays of my upper and lower abdomen. The porter who took me down to x-ray was a pastor of a Pentecostal church, and he had the joy of the Lord in him. We talked constantly about the goodness of our Lord Jesus and how great and loving He is toward His children. When we got to x-ray, there was another young black man with a shiny, beautiful face and I knew right away that he had Jesus in his life.

The three of us prayed together and rebuked the cancerous tumor in my body, and God's peace and anointing came down upon us at that moment. It was amazing how God had put these two gentlemen in my life at that very time when I needed them most. I just cried and said to them how much I love Jesus and how it is amazing that they were in a position to be a comfort to me and to others around them in time of need. It was a very joyous occasion, and one I won't forget for a very long time. God is good, and his love for His children is amazing, even for me.

Emil came to visit me Friday evening after work and spent forty-five minutes chatting; it was lovely to see him there. I unfortunately did not see Dr. Abulafi on that Friday but was reassured I would see him on Saturday when he made his hospital rounds.

On Saturday morning, I got up early again and went to have a shower. It was lovely to feel a bit normal again, and the pain was easing so I was in great spirits when I woke up praising the Lord for another day. Every morning I pray for grace, health, strength, joy, and life in my body before I leave for the office and when I get up generally. It is so important to pray as soon as you get up as it is the beginning of the day, and you need His blood covering you throughout the day. There is no point just praying at night; it's too late. Don't get me wrong; pray at night as well as in the morning. In fact, the Bible says to pray unceasingly.

Rita, a Lithuanian lady opposite me, had her appendix removed, and she was recovering from that surgery. She and I hit it off right away, and on Saturday morning after breakfast we went for a long walk around the corridors. I showed her all the places I would walk in my recovery last year. We even went to see the children's ward and walked past the dreaded operating theaters.

After my sandwich and soup for lunch on Saturday, three of us were relaxing by my bed talking about nothing when Dr. Abulafi arrived with his assistant. It was great to see him, and I felt reassured that at least something was being done. He closed the curtains around my bed and did an examination of my abdomen. He sat down on my bed and was very sympathetic with my pain. I did tell him that I was taking pain killers every time the nurses came around the wards to administer drugs to patients. He mentioned that he had received a fax just yesterday with how the doctors were going to proceed with my treatment—hot off the press!

Unfortunately it was going to be a very complex operation as the tumor *had* invaded the bladder. What this meant was that he now needed to build a team around him that was going to perform the operation. This would include a team of plastic surgeons from St. George's Hospital in Tooting along with himself and doctors from Royal Marsden. They would need to cut off a segment of my bladder and remove the tumor and replace the bladder part with a plastic flap. To be honest, ignorance is bliss, and I would prefer not to know what was involved. My theory is not to tell me the details, just do it as God has given these doctors an amazing gift, and whatever comes my way is God's will and ultimately He is in control.

Dr. Abulafi said that getting the right teams together was going to take some time and that in the interim we needed to manage my pain. The surprising thing was that he said that I could stay at the hospital for them to manage the pain for however long, or I could go home and manage the pain. I of course jumped at going home. He assured me that I would be getting strong pain killers to take with me and that I should use them whenever needed. I was so excited that I at least knew the course of action to be taken. The cystoscopy would be done sooner rather than later. The doctor had spoken to the urology department himself, and I would hear about the date within the week.

While we were talking, another doctor came and took some blood from me—another needle! Dr. Abulafi said that I would be discharged once they saw if the bloodwork was okay. I was happy to be discharged.

I was upset that it was going to be a complex operation, and I also forgot to ask whether they could do the stoma reversal at the same time. When you are with doctors on your own and don't have a husband to remind you of things to ask, then you tend to forget things. Never mind, I am not going to dwell on the worst-case scenario. God has a plan in my life, and He knows the bigger picture. I don't.

I could not wait for Emil to get back to the hospital for the 2:00 p.m. visiting hours. I was so annoyed with him that he only got to the hospital at 2:45 p.m. I forgot that I had said that he must come later on Saturday as he would be with me pretty much all afternoon and evening. That is not the point—he should have been there at 2:00! It was lovely to see him, and we went for a walk downstairs to Costa Coffee where I had my first decent cup of coffee since entering the emergency room on Thursday. I explained to Emil what Dr. Abulafi had said and he seemed reassured as well that everything possible was being done for me.

We went back upstairs, and Sharon, one of the ladies on the ward, mentioned that the doctor who took the blood came around to give me my discharge letter. I could not believe that everything was working so quickly; usually you have to wait hours to be discharged. I went around to the nurses' station, and the doctor was there. She mentioned that my blood platelets were low and that I would need to go to my local general practioner's (GP) practice to get blood tests done within a week or two; otherwise I was discharged. One of the nurses gave me a bag full of medication/pain killers to take home with me, along with some laxatives in order for my stoma to work properly.

I went back to the ward, got dressed into my work clothes I had worn Thursday when I went to the emergency room, I did look like a bit of a Charlie, but I was definitely the smartest patient leaving the hospital that day. I went around the ward, saying my farewells to all the ladies and giving a big hug to Rita; she was leaving shortly after me. I went to the nurse's station and said my farewells and finally got rid of the dreaded cannula that was in my arm since Thursday night. There had been an amazing Indian couple in Queens 1 who every morning early came in and shouted good morning and had the biggest smiles on their faces. I remembered them from my last visit, and they always lifted the ladies spirits. They would bring us tea or coffee in the early morning; provide our meals, and put fresh water in our bedside cabinets. This amazing NHS staff is so often forgotten but such a vital part of the healing process, and I cannot thank them enough for their joyous spirits.

Emil and I got home around 6:00 on Saturday night, and I can't tell you how excited and happy I was to be home—albeit a rental place. Emil and I had dinner at home and watched a movie before I took a couple of pain killers and went to sleep. I have to admit that before going to sleep I had a moment where I was just so angry with the Lord. I completely lost the plot and sobbed and pleaded with the Lord to help me; I could not take any more of the pain and further operations and hospital stays. I wanted out, I wanted my life back, and I wanted to forget the whole thing happened. I know it sounds silly, but I got to a stage where everything just boiled over in that moment, and I totally lost the plot. After a while I calmed down, prayed to God for peace, and went to bed relatively early as I knew Sunday was going to be busy with church.

Chapter Ten

Life at Home 2

*O*n Sunday, May 4, I was overjoyed to be able to attend my church and fellowship with my family. We had an amazing message from God: "Keep the Faith" that seemed to be just for me. After church, Emil and I walked down to Oxford Street and saw a lovely pub on the way, where the sun was shining with lovely plants and an extensive burger menu. I did say nothing was wrong with my appetite. We ordered a couple of wine spritzers and sat in the sun for a couple of hours, eating and drinking and enjoying the spring sunshine. We then proceeded down to John Lewis to pick up some wallpaper we had ordered for our new flat.

Well, John Lewis was an experience. When we arrived, there were so many people and the heating was on high. We went up to the Haberdashery department, and all I can remember is seeing some massive Mr. Blobby or some other character dressed up and walking the aisles. All of a sudden, I seemed to have bounced off him and faint flat on my bum in the aisle in the middle of a crowded department store. I next came around with Emil joking with the sales assistant and telling her to carry my handbag as it did not suit him carrying it. Needless to say, all I wanted to do was get out of there and not feel as if everyone was looking at me. We hurriedly got the wallpaper and departed after I was given a nice glass of cold water. I cannot recall ever fainting in my life before this illness, but nowadays I seem to be doing it quite frequently, which is very embarrassing.

Monday was a bank holiday, and my sister, Jessica, came around. We spent the day inside eating and watching movies. Poor Emil was doing all the running around after us, which was lovely. I definitely believe there is a crown in glory waiting for him.

On Tuesday morning, I was so excited to get back to work, and I wanted to surprise everyone that I was back. Well, I think the surprise was on me; the company had booked a temp in for the week, thinking I was not going to be fit enough to work. I was devastated! After doing a handover, I left after lunch and went back home, disappointed that they had found someone to replace me so quickly.

On Thursday morning, I got a call from my boss which was a nice surprise. He mentioned that the management team had a meeting, and they all decided it was best that I stay home and return after my forthcoming operation and recovery. To be honest, I was once more absolutely devastated. We "had a domestic" for a good ten minutes about why I wanted to get back. I tried to explain that it was the only thing that got me up in the mornings, and it brought a bit of normalcy back in my life. I did not want to stay home and have to think about things and look at four walls all day. I was tearful but understood that they might be awkward asking me to do things for them, although that was totally not my intention. I did not need sympathy; I just wanted my life back. Anyway, I lost the argument and now I am at home watching God TV, writing this book, and eating loads of food. I very much appreciate their love and thoughtfulness but so miss working and my work colleagues.

When I went back to the office for the month the company took out a "critical illness" policy for all staff. Thank God I went back when I did; now I am being paid 75 percent of my salary by UNUM indefinitely. I have not lost a day's pay since my illness kicked in. The owner had been amazing and had paid my full salary since I became ill, and now UNUM is paying. Thank you, Jesus, for your provision and blessings.

After chasing various doctors, secretaries, and whomever else I thought could help, I finally got an appointment letter in the mail for my cystoscopy. The procedure was scheduled for May 21 and would take place at the Croydon University Hospital. Finally, I had a date nearly a whole month after Dr. Abulafi requested it. I was on their urgent list, which apparently had a waiting time of between four to six weeks. I could not believe it! To be honest, I think some patients must die before they have some appointments because of the amount of waiting that takes place between different departments.

On Tuesday, May 13, I called Ramani at Royal Marsden to let her know that I was no longer working and also to see if she had any news about my case. She mentioned that a letter had just been faxed to Royal Marsden in Chelsea to ask them to take on my case as I had been referred to them by Croydon University Hospital. In a way I was a bit upset that Dr. Abulafi, my consultant at Croydon University Hospital, was not going to perform the operation, but all kudos to him, he felt it would be best for Marsden with advanced knowledge of complex cases to deal with this. In a way I was relieved as well; I would now be dealing with one hospital where Ramani was a part of a team, and hopefully things might be a lot quicker moving forward with various appointments.

On Thursday, May 15, I called Dr. Rasheed's medical assistant at Marsden in Chelsea to try and make an appointment and hopefully speed up the process as she would have received the referral letter by fax on Tuesday. Dr. Rasheed was going to be the overall surgeon in charge of my upcoming operation at RMH. I spoke to her, and what a lovely lady she is. She mentioned that she had just posted my appointment letter and that I was to come to Chelsea on Friday, May 23—what a relief. I just prayed to God that everything now would move forward really fast.

The next week would be busy with various hospital appointments. On Monday, I needed to go to CUH to see the anesthetist, on Wednesday I would go down for my cystoscopy, and on Friday I would go to Marsden in Chelsea to see Dr. Rasheed.

May 19 finally came, after much angst I have to say. This cystoscopy test I had to be the most frustrating thing I have ever done in my life. Initially on April 23, I was told that an MRI and cystoscopy would be done within a couple of weeks. Well, the MRI was done within a couple of days by Marsden, but the cystoscopy has been a night-mare. I had chased until I was blue in the face. Initially I was able to secure a cancellation appointment for May 24 (after saying my case was urgent and needed to be done within two weeks of April 23, which was frightening!)

After my hospital visit and seeing Dr. Abulafi, he chased Urology, and he was able to secure an appointment for May 21 (3 days earlier but better than nothing). Anyway, on the weekend before the Monday when I was due to be in to have my pre-admission tests, I got another letter in the mail to say that my cystoscopy has been moved to the Thursday, June 5. Well, I can tell you I was upset to say the least. I could not believe after all my chasing and Dr. Abulafi's, they could move it back three weeks. I could not sleep that night and waited for Monday morning to see what was going on. After many phone calls, they finally agreed to keep my original appointments and apologized.

My main concern is for old folks suffering cancer on their own and who don't have the will to fight for what is their right to good treatment and quick appointments. I think the main difference between Marsden and Croydon University Hospital is that CUH treats everyone, regardless of illness, all the same, whereas Marsden is strictly a cancer hospital and fasttracks everyone, as time is of the essence in most cases.

Monday, May 19, I went in for pre-admissions tests which involved an ECG and MRSA and blood tests, which were very fast and painless. Also, a load of health questionnaires had to be filled in. I met a number of nurses who were Christians, and what a blessing they were to me and a shining light to all.

On Wednesday, May 21, I went with Jessica to the hospital for my cystoscopy. I was so relieved that it was actually going ahead; I could not believe it. The fact that we had to wait three hours to be admitted to the theater was immaterial. The urologist performing the operation was a lovely young man who mentioned that they would be putting a camera in my bladder to see what damage had been caused, as well as putting dye in my tubes leading to my kidneys to see if there were any blockages; if so, they would put a stent in to help the forthcoming operation. I prayed quietly and said that the medically impossible is going to happen and that there would be no damage to the bladder and all clear with the tubes.

I was wheeled into the pre-operation theater where the anesthetist and various nurses were preparing me. Did I mention I hate needles! Well, the anesthetist took three tries to find a vein; it was very painful the first time, but after that I just prayed and said that this was nothing compared to what the Lord suffered on the cross for me. It worked; it was relatively painless and within seconds I had fallen asleep, which was lovely.

I woke up in the recovery ward and the urologist was shaking me awake. He mentioned that the procedure went well and that the inner wall of the bladder had not been intruded by the tumor, but the outer wall had and that the tubes to the kidneys were all clear. I gave him a huge hug and thanked the Lord for his mercies. I needed to use the ladies facilities before I left the hospital as the nurses like to see people's plumbing all working and in order before they depart. I was warned that I might have a lot of blood and be in some considerable pain for the first passing of water. Well, thank you, Lord, I had none of the above. At this stage, all I could think about was food. I was absolutely famished. It was literally twenty-four hours since I had eaten, and for me that is a very long time—I love my food. The hospital kindly gave me a sandwich and a lovely cup of tea. Jessica was waiting outside, and we gave each other a hug and thanked God all the way home. Of course we had to stop off and get some Ben & Jerry's ice cream to celebrate the good news.

On Friday, May 23, I popped into work to drop off a cake I had baked for everyone. It was lovely seeing most of the folk and having a good laugh. I picked up Emil from his office around the corner, and we made our way to the Royal Marsden in Chelsea. I had an appointment with my new consultant surgeon at 3:00 p.m. We arrived early and fortunately were able to see him a half hour earlier than scheduled, which was great. I find these days, the shorter time I spend in hospitals the better. This was our first visit to the Chelsea Marsden, and I must say that some of the people we saw were desperately frail and ill. I find myself just pleading the blood of Jesus over everyone I see; it really breaks my heart.

We met Dr. Rasheed who is a very knowledgeable, clued-up young man who knew everything about my case, which was reassuring. He walked into the room with no notes but just started drawing loads of diagrams, explaining what I had been through and what I was going to have to go through. When he started on the gory details, I asked if I could be excused, I am a total believer in ignorance is bliss and leaving it up to the knowledgeable doctors and the Lord Jesus Christ to sort out. I know it is a cop-out, but it has worked for me so far and thank the Lord his healing power after the last operation has been awesome. God uses the doctors as his instruments here on earth to heal the sick, and God's healing power is with them and with me. I am a testimony to that—absolutely.

Unfortunately, Dr. Rasheed wanted me to listen to everything as he said that 90 percent success of an operation is in the preparation and that all patients need to know what they are getting themselves into. I so did not want to hear but had no choice. The long and short of it is that the tumor had not invaded the inner wall of my bladder, which was amazing, and thank you, Jesus, just the outside wall, as all the scans had indicated. However, the tumor is pressing into the pubic bone so they will need to cut off a section of the pubic bone—seriously, all I could think of was in the medieval times how they would operate on people with saws, hammers, and chisels. I really did not want to hear that.

He mentioned that the pain would need to be managed, so if I needed stronger stuff like morphine, then I needed to get the tablets from my doctor whenever I required them. To be honest, my God is bigger than any pain tablets. He does not realize that I have not been taking any pain tablets whatsoever, and that I am walking in the shadow of the Almighty, trusting for pain relief—and it is working, so no tablets for me. Thank you.

Before leaving the hospital, I of course had to give yet more blood samples, which meant another needle—hooray! We left the hospital, and I must say I felt rather deflated and really did not want to hear all the information that was provided. He mentioned that the operation should happen within the next three or four weeks or as soon as he can get the various plastic surgeons, urologist, and so forth together. Then it was a waiting game, and I was trusting that the operation will happen sooner rather than later.

The great news is that I had booked the Grace and Faith 2014 Conference a few weeks back. It is a Christian conference held annually in Telford where Andrew Wommack Ministries run the event. Jessica, Emil, and I left early Saturday morning, and trust me; I know all the service station facilities along the M40. Departing during the London bank holiday was an absolute nightmare and a journey that should have taken three hours lasted six and a half. We finally arrived at our destination safe and in time for the Saturday evening service. I cannot tell you how perfect the message was for me at that specific moment in my life. Faith brings about grace and just reiterating the goodness of the Lord Jesus is exactly what I needed to hear: no thinking about carnal doctor's diagnosis but the supernatural power of our God. I went up for prayer afterward, knowing that the good work had started in my life and the wonder-working power of our Lord Jesus was and is upon me. Amen!

In the difficult moments when the storms of life hit us in various ways, be it emotional, physical, or financial, it is hard to walk by faith and not by sight. Paul was mentioned and how he suffered for Christ. Paul was left for dead; he was imprisoned, stoned, shipwrecked three times, and whipped five times, and he yet said, "Rejoice in the Lord always, and again I say rejoice." Job was of similar character; his friends around him dissuaded him and were definitely not encouraging, but yet Job loved the Lord God, and after his hardships were over everything he lost was returned to him multiplied.

So, I won't lie to you, I have for the past couple of days been feeling very tired and in a little pain. I tend to sing and worship to the Lord and try to not focus on what my body is feeling. I have nothing to complain about after reading the hardships and trials God's disciples had to go through. God never promised a bed of roses, but He did say He would never leave us or forsake us and I can testify to God's mercies every day I am alive.

Chapter Eleven

Hospital Holiday Camp 3

*O*n the bank holiday Monday we arrived back from the Andrew Wommack conference, I was not feeling all too great. At first I thought it might have been the long road trip or the long meetings I had sat through. Come Thursday, I was busy climbing walls with the pain. I have never felt so much pain like this. It was very similar to the pain I felt back in July when I was rushed into the emergency room on my first incident. A couple of times during the week, I had called my clinical nurse at the Royal Marsden to ask for advice on the pain, and she recommended that I see my GP for an assessment. I was not too sure what the GP could do, but I called the office late Thursday afternoon for an emergency appointment at 9:20 a.m. on Friday.

On Friday, May 30, I arrived at the doctor's office in much pain and walking like the hunchback of Notre

Dame. I finally got in to see the doctor, who was not my usual doctor who was on vacation. She was a very young doctor, and I went in to the consultation room feeling very skeptical about what she could do for me. We had to run through my notes about my history, and then I had to pop onto the table for an examination. Unfortunately, she could not even touch my left side of my tummy as I was in too much pain. I think that my case overwhelmed her, and she said that she was unable to do anything for me herself. She was very kind indeed, and called the surgical team at Croydon University Hospital (CUH) as well as the Royal Marsden Hospital (RMH) to explain what she had found. There was some swelling on my left side and unusual coloring around my stoma, along with my intense pain.

Ten minutes later, an ambulance arrived at the doctor's office and took me to the emergency room at CUH where tests were done on me and the medical team plied me with morphine—lovely. One of the doctors mentioned to me that the pain was caused by scar tissue that looked as though it was wrapping around the colon, which meant they may have to do an emergency operation on me. I was scared and right away turned to the Lord Jesus Christ and rebuked that comment. I did however mention that if the operation was required, then they needed to speak to the Royal Marsden in Chelsea first, as I had an operation lined up with them at the end of the month. I was then wheeled in for a CT scan and waited for the results of the scan. At this stage, my brother and my niece arrived, which was a lovely surprise. Emil had called to ask if they wouldn't mind staying with me, and he would try and leave work in the early evening so he could be with me. I asked my brother and Gemma, my niece, to pray that I would not need this stupid operation they were talking about.

Praise the Lord! The results came back, and the colon had not wrapped itself around the scar tissue, but the discomfort was due to scar tissue. I was then wheeled up to Queens 1 (the same ward I had been in twice previously)—in the same window bed I had stayed in previously. Isn't God merciful? I was so happy to see all the usual nurses again. Most of them are from the Philippines, and what a lovely bunch of ladies they are. By this time I was absolutely starving. I think I had a cup of tea and a sandwich brought to me around 3:3:00 p.m., and at 5:00, I received a much welcome plate of lasagna. The Lord knows I love food, and throughout my illness I have not been put off food, which has been amazing. My weight had gone up as well, and I was weighing 117lbs, so I have put on a fair amount since I was discharged from hospital the last time.

At midnight on Friday evening, the three night nurses on duty came to my bed and said that the Royal Marsden had requested they put a catheter in me and also a tube down my nose and throat to my tummy to relieve some of the pressure. To be honest, I knew what a catheter was, but the tube was a mystery; I was not sure what they were talking about—just as well! I had to sit up and the nurses struggled at first to put this long, see-through tube down my nose. I was not sure what they were trying to do, but then they tried the other nostril and the tube went down, through my nose, throat, and finally into my tummy. All the time, one of the nurses was giving me a straw and water to drink while this was going on. I cannot tell you how uncomfortable the whole scenario was and how I felt like gagging constantly with this thing in my throat. I was just focusing on Paul and Job and all the trials they had to go through and thinking this was nothing—get a grip and stop being a drama queen.

I finally managed to get a couple of hours' sleep afterward and woke up in the morning on Saturday, feeling decidedly uncomfortable and then realizing why. Unfortunately, once they had put the tube down me, I was to have "nil by mouth" (NBM). Darn, I maybe should have had a lot more to eat the night before. By midmorning I had a visit from Dr. Abulafi's registrar who was very nice and sympathetic and mentioned that RMH was trying to find a bed and that I should not hold out much hope about being transferred until the next day. Please God, I just wanted to get to RMH and get this tube out as soon as possible. By lunch time, while everyone was eating their lunches, I was lying in bed and the consultant surgeon on call came round. She was a middle-aged Indian lady who was very clued up and knew what she wanted. She came to my bed and said that I would be transferred to RMH today and told the CUH registrar to let the RMH registrar make plans and get it done. Amazing, she was like a guardian angel that swept in and out and got things done for my benefit—thank you, Lord.

On Saturday at 1:30 p.m., the ambulance crew came to the ward to pick me up and take me to RMH in Chelsea. What a lovely set of guys they were, very considerate and patient. We got chatting on the way down to the ambulance, and I mentioned I would need to call my husband to tell him not to come to CUH to visit but make his way to RMH in Chelsea. The ambulance crew then asked me where I lived and when I explained the location, they said they would pick Emil up outside our flat and take us both up to London. I could not believe how God was just moving everyone and setting everything in motion perfectly.

We met Emil outside the flat and made our way to London. Over an hour later, we arrived at RMH—well, we thought it was the RMH. I did not realize that there are a couple of other hospitals right next door to the RMH (Royal Brompton and the Imperial Hospital). Unfortunately the ambulance driver was not too sure where he was going, and we went to the first reception area we found and asked for the Ellis Ward. We were told the fifth floor, where we made our way up but could only see the Elizabeth Ward. We then realized that we were at the Royal Brompton Hospital and not the RMH. All four of us sheepishly exited and made our way outside to find the RMH. All this time I have a mini-entourage with me, sitting in a wheelchair being pushed by a paramedic and Emil and another paramedic following. We went through back streets and over speed bumps trying to find the RMH reception. I had a quiet chuckle inside thinking I could make a "Carry On" movie about this little episode. There I am in my hospital nightie and blanket dodging cars and speed bumps trying to find the right hospital. I can't say it was the most scenic way to approach the Marsden as we arrived via a parking lot and through the back door.

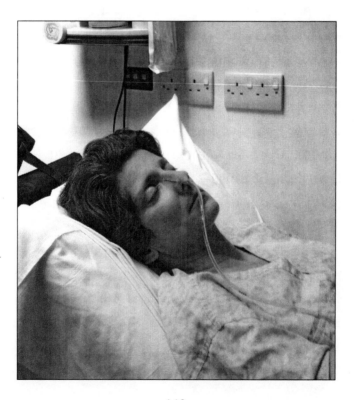

We finally found the RMH, only to find we were locked out of the ambulance entrance for some reason. Fortunately a lovely nurse arrived, and she let us in and actually took us to the Ellis Ward. Wow! The ward was amazing. I learned later that one of the patients had left some money in her will for the Ellis Ward to be refurbished in her favorite colors, and you could definitely see a designer had got in and finished it out to a beautiful standard. The showers were lovely as well and fully functioning. What a difference a lovely environment makes to patients at this trying time. The paramedics were blown away, as well, by the luxury and thoughtfulness of the whole place. What was also amazing was that each bed had a lovely TV monitor which you did not have to pay for—not like most hospitals. You could definitely see the difference in hospital standards between CUH and RMH. It is a shame that the standard of luxury varies so hugely between hospitals, although the care is the same.

By the time I settled down, it was late Saturday afternoon just in time to be told that Dr. Rasheed, my consultant, was on call that weekend, and he would be visiting me shortly. Can you believe how God is in control of all things—amazing! I saw Dr. Rasheed, and he prescribed me various painkillers and said that I would be in the RMH for a good five or six days to be monitored and to try and control the pain. I was comfortable with that as I knew I was in good hands at the RMH and with my Maker. I think

I realized this was my first step towards full healing and recovery in Jesus' name.

Sunday was very nice as I still could not eat due to still having the horrible tube down my throat, but I was expecting Emil to come in the afternoon along with my ex-boss from Miami who was visiting London with his wife. We had actually arranged to have lunch with them on the Sunday prior to my having been taken to hospital, so I was really looking forward to seeing them again. By the afternoon, I also had Nick and Jessica come, as well, and we had lovely fellowship around my bed. Unfortunately, the tube was so annoying me, and I could not speak for too long and of course still had nothing to eat—I was starving. All I could think about was naughty food treats and what my first meal was going to be.

On Monday, June 9, early in the morning, Dr. Rasheed came to see me before he went into surgery. I must say, when I first met him we hit it off right away. He is young and very funny and has a great bedside manner and a fantastic sense of humor. By this time I was so desperate to get the tube out of my system, I asked if he could please do the honors, which he did. No more catheter and no more tubes—thank you, Jesus. What a relief to actually be able to swallow normally and be able to do my favorite pastime—*talk*!

On Monday, I was able to have a shower, and I felt great afterwards, like a new woman. Unfortunately, I was still on fluids, which I had to finish by lunchtime Monday. So there I was in the shower, one arm out trying to preserve the cannula in my arm where the various drugs were being pumped. As you all know, I hate needles; my worst nightmare would be for yet another injection to put another cannula in my arm. Every night for the duration of your stay in the hospital, patients have to have an injection either in their upper arm or thigh to prevent blood coagulation. So by the time you leave hospital, you definitely are covered in bruises and look like a pin cushion. The first few days that I had the tube down me, they put paracetamol through the cannula into my veins. They tried once to put Tramadol (really strong painkiller like morphine) into my veins, but only finished half the dosage, and then I was as sick as a dog. Afterward, they injected me with various other painkillers to see which one worked best for me. RMH has a dedicated team of nurses who solely control pain for patients, which is unbelievable. Each patient has a pain killer regime as a standing order that has been worked out by this team, and they are amazing and very caring.

On Monday afternoon, after having my first meal since Friday evening, it was lovely to have some beautifully cooked fish and mashed potatoes. The RMH have an amazing menu, compared to other hospitals. I did not sample the breakfast menu, but you could have a full English as well as scrambled eggs, omelet, or the usual toast and cereal. It was amazing the choice of foods that were presented on a daily basis. It is such a shame that the regular NHS hospitals are not all decorated and furnished out like the RMH, as it would make a huge difference to the patients' well-being. Mental note: if I ever come into some money I would definitely "do out" Queens 1 at CUH. The morale of patients as well as staff must surely be affected by the surroundings they work in.

I had my pastor surprise me with a visit Monday afternoon. What a joy to see him and speak to him about the Lord's goodness and mercies. We spent some time in the patients' lounge and then gave him a copy of Andrew Wommack's book *God Wants You Well* to give to Gina, another cancer sufferer in our church whom Pastor Bill was seeing later on in the week. Seeing my pastor there gave me a huge boost and a new vigor to fight the fight with faith and grace. Satan had no stronghold over me; my body was the Lord's, and everything inside was His to perform a mighty miracle. Amen.

On Tuesday morning the "bladder man" or that is what I call him anyway, came to my bed and started explaining what he was going to do in the operation. Dr. Kumar was his name, and he was unbelievably young but very clever. To be honest, I told him I would rather not have any gory details but trusted him to do his best and left it at that. Dr. Rasheed then came and had a quick meeting with me and said that it looks like the pain has been managed and that he would stop by on Thursday morning with the plastic surgeon. He did warn me that the plastic surgeon was very good looking—I always joke with Dr. Rasheed how young and good-looking the doctors are, so it is a running joke between us.

Unfortunately the Tramadol painkillers made me constipated. For the past couple of days, I had been having a bowl of prunes and fruit yogurt for breakfast and also a couple of Laxido sachets a day. At that moment in time I has to try and manage my pain along with staying hydrated and frequent—if you know what I mean. I did ask the nurse to stop the Tramadol and just give me paracetamol for the next couple of days. I had also been prescribed antibiotics as I seemed to have a urinary infection. Oh well, it could be worse.

Very early on Thursday, June 5, Dr. Ramsey, the plastic surgeon, along with a team of doctors and Dr. Rasheed came to my bed, and we discussed a few things before he had a look at my tummy. He also asked if he could see my upper leg. I am not too sure why, but thank goodness I had shaved before coming into hospital (a girl has to think of these things). He then mentioned that he needs to cut into where my six pack lies at the bottom of my pelvis and remove the tumor and try and connect the muscles back together again. If he is unable to stretch the muscles then he would need to cut a piece of skin off my thigh and place it between the muscles. He also briefly skimmed over the pubic bone and bladder scenario and what he was going to do. I did mention to him beforehand that I did not want any gory details, just the bare necessities. All of them confirmed that the operation date would be more than likely June 26, depending on bed availability in the ICU/HDU. My faith is in the Lord and all His ways— He knows the bigger picture, and it seems like I will be having a fantastic, young, dynamic team in the operating theater, and of course the Great Physician—wow, I could not be in a better place than that. I am looking forward to the healing process afterward and the peace and joy that comes with it.

The team then left my bedside and a minute later Dr. Rasheed came running back and said to me, "I told you he was good looking." Dr. Rasheed was certainly not wrong—if I was twenty years younger. Dr. Rasheed asked if I wanted to go home today or tomorrow; I definitely said today. I couldn't wait to get out and see Emil and get home to a bit of normalcy. Visiting hours in the RMH are fantastic, they are between 8:00 a.m. and 12:00 p.m. and then from 2:00 p.m. to 8:00 p.m. So, the hours are much longer than the regular NHS hospitals, but one thing I have noticed is that the visitors at RMH are very respectful and quiet. I also strongly believe that the RMH environment plays a huge part in visitors behaving well and patients recovering quicker.

On Thursday, there were three of us leaving the ward at the same time, and we were asked to go to the visitors lounge by 10:00 a.m. so the beds could be made for the new arrivals. We all waited in the lounge until our medicines were dispensed and then left around 11:00 a.m. I managed to get a bus to Victoria Station and then a train onto East Croydon without too much inconvenience. Emil wanted to pick me up from the hospital that evening, but I could not hang around the hospital for that long. It was fantastic to be home, and I unpacked right away and started doing a bit of dusting and put a load of clothes in the washing machine—back to normalcy in no time.

So now, I am at home taking just the paracetamol for the meantime and trusting the Lord that will be enough. I would rather have my stoma work than anything else. I need to take the antibiotics for a week, and then I have the all-clear down below. I must now manage my pain and will need to do a couple of up-to-date scans for Dr. Rasheed before the operation—bring it on! The good thing is that I saw all the various surgeons while I was in hospital so no office visits for me—hallelujah!

Chapter Twelve

The Big One

A few days after returning from the hospital I received a number of letters from RMH requesting I come in the week commencing June 16 for various scans. On June 18, I had been requested to go to RMH for a CT scan, June 19 for an MRI scan, and on Friday, June 20, for a two-hour pre-op assessment. Fortunately, I got a phone call on the June 17 to say that there was no need to come in for the CT scan as I had just had one a month ago—thank you, Lord.

During my MRI scan, it was rather embarrassing but I did wait until the noise subsided between scans. I had to press the emergency button on the side of the bed, as the panel the nurses had put on my tummy was really painful from the pressure and fortunately they put sponges between my tummy and the scan panel—whew! The nurses had also given me an injection of Buscopan to relax my bowels so I was also pleased to get to the ladies' room once the scan had finished. The most basic of things now seems such an ordeal. Oh well; it will soon be all over.

On Friday, I had to do an ECG, blood pressure, weight and height measurements, and meet the anesthetist, and of course the dreaded blood tests. I had a lovely nurse doing all the various tests with me, and we of course got chatting away; unfortunately, after she had removed the needle and filled three of the little tubes with blood, we both noticed that she had not filled the fourth one. We looked at each other, and my heart sank. We had talked so much we were clearly not paying enough attention. She kindly reassured me that she would put some of the blood from the others into the fourth and send them off and see what the results come back with. One half-hour later, she came back and apologized, I had to have another blood sample taken. Before I could even think about it she had stuck the needle in the same hole as the last one—ouch! It serves me right for talking so much.

I was really pleased that I had put on weight, a whole 2.2lbs since I left the hospital last month and now weighed a healthy 119lbs, despite all my pigging out. I have been consciously trying to eat loads before the operation and build up my energy. This included a lot of unhealthy food I would never normally dream of eating. I am probably overexaggerating that they are really unhealthy foods, but they would not normally be what we ate. I am also addicted to frozen yogurt; I really don't know why.

The anesthetist was very nice—I must say I have been most impressed with the whole team that will be performing the operation. The anesthetist started going into a long discussion about what he was going to do and of course I asked him not to. Unfortunately, he has to tell me what the plans will be, including an epidural. Oh man, are you kidding me that is one big needle going into my spine—marvelous; I can't wait! I of course asked not to have it done, but he did stress that the operation was going to be very painful, and it would help with easing of this when I woke up in ICU. I said to him that I trust him to do the best, the team, and the man upstairs to get me through this and that healing comes swiftly. My prayer is still that once they go in, they will see that the tumor has disintegrated and they can do the reversal of my stoma— all things are possible.

The anesthetist also mentioned that I would be in ICU for two days and then followed by ten days in the Ellis Ward recouping. He could not tell me how long the operation would be but that I would need to be at the hospital at 7:30 a.m. on Thursday, June 26, and they would commence the operation around 8:30. I just hope that all the surgeons have had a strong cup of coffee and they are all in good moods that early in the morning. I have so many friends and family praying for me, and I know that the blood of Jesus is going to cover me and that the surgeons will have steady hands and the operations will not be as complex as what they expected, in Jesus' name—amen!

As a Christian I am finding myself more and more having spiritual warfare on my mind. The devil is very clever when it comes to being a liar and being deceitful. Before my operation, he was giving me such negative thoughts and making me think the worst-case scenario. Well, the devil is not going to win this little lady; I belong to the Lord Jesus Christ. It brings the story of Adam and Eve so alive when you think about spiritual warfare and bad thoughts. The devil never forced Adam and Eve to have any of the forbidden fruit, but he very subtly coerced and persuaded them that it was the best thing for them. The devil has no power over us, he is a defeated foe—like an annoying little bug that keeps coming back and back until we succumb. As Christians we need to know when the little bug is talking to us, and we need to trod on it and rebuke it in Jesus name. We need to stand on the promises of what the word of God says and not succumb to temptation from the devil.

Emil and I got up at 5:00 a.m. on Thursday, June 26, and I had a quick shower before we left for RMH in Chelsea. I am absolutely buzzing and so excited that this day has finally come. We got the early train from East Croydon to London Victoria and then the underground to South Kensington and a short walk to RMH. We were half an hour early, arriving at 7:00. Unfortunately, we were told that an emergency operation needed to be performed before mine and that I would probably go into the theater around 11:00. I would of course have preferred not to wait, and get the whole thing done sooner rather than later, but it was nice to talk with Emil beforehand. All the surgeons who were going to be in the operation came to visit me and reassured me that everything was in place. The plastic surgeon mentioned that they would be also putting in a synthetic mesh into my tummy, which would replace the tumor and give me some form. The bladder outer wall would be getting a cap and the pubic bone will be cut and capped. All the time he is telling me what he plans to do I was rebuking it in Jesus' name. I told him that what he is saying won't happen; it will be a very easy operation for him.

Before Dr. Ramsey arrived, one of the nurses gave me a hospital gown to get into and mentioned that I needed to have the opening of the gown in the front and that when Dr. Ramsey came I just needed to open the gown, and he would mark my breasts. I looked at her rather dumbfounded and mentally going over why he would mark my breasts. I then realized, Dr. Ramsey, the cute plastic surgeon, also did reconstruction of breasts. I told the nurse that it was not my breasts being operated on but my pelvis. We both had a good giggle. It would have been so funny, the cute plastic surgeon coming through the curtains, me, a desperate old lady exposing myself and thinking what is wrong. Oh well, this story is better said rather than written, but very funny nonetheless.

By 10:30, I was asked to walk down to the operating theater as they were ready for me. I was very nervous but praying the whole time and squeezing Emil's hand and reassuring him all will be fine. I left Emil at the doors and went into the cavernous basement of the RMH where all the operating theaters are. I think I counted a total of ten theaters' it's amazing; you would never think there was such a rabbit warren of operating theaters in the basement. I was guided into Theater 6's pre-operating theater where the anesthetist was waiting, along with a few other nurses. I looked behind the anesthetist's head and noticed a window into the actual operating theater where I would soon be. It looked like a movie set with the lights on above the heads of surgeons, their heads bent down, peering into somebody's open torso. It was not something I really wanted to see before I went under, but nevertheless we had a bit of a laugh before they put the needle in and I went off to the land of nod.

Around 6:00 p.m., I woke up in ICU and saw a couple of nurses by my bedside, Louise and Chris. What an amazing pair of dedicated young nurses. Emil was also there, looking rather relieved that the whole thing was over. Emil also could not believe what he was about to tell me; he was so happy. Apparently my bladder was not affected in any way, and the tumor had peeled away from the bladder like a Satsuma. Thank you, Jesus, that is totally a prayer answered, and I just wanted to shout and scream and do cartwheels. Throughout, all the scans had shown that the outer wall of the bladder was intruded on. Well, the Lord has done it again! Why do I ever doubt His goodness?

Of course, ICU was how I remembered it, loads of monitors, lights and beeping noises throughout the day, but really a place where you are well looked after. I am not too sure when Emil left as I was still on cloud nine with all the morphine they were giving me, but the following morning, Friday, June 27, I woke up in ICU feeling remarkably relaxed and in not so much pain at all. Friday was a total blur; all I could remember was nurses rushing around and monitoring various people. By 7:00 that evening, I was wheeled down to the Ellis Ward, where I had been previously. It was bizarre; it was like visiting old acquaintances as everyone recognized me from my previous stay around five weeks prior. I was relieved to be back in Ellis Ward and knew that my recovery was beginning.

Saturday, June 28, needless to say, was a most relaxing day in bed ever. Emil came to visit Saturday afternoon, and he looked exhausted. Emil's brother, Armen, was flying in from L.A. early Monday morning so Emil was preparing for his visit as well as visiting me—bless him. Armen was going to spend the following week spending time with me

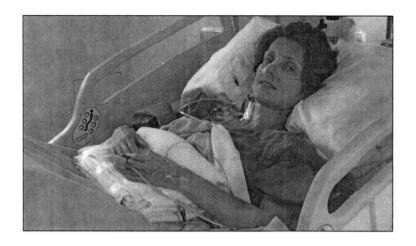

in hospital and entertaining his brother in the evenings. Unfortunately, it was month's end at Emil's company, so he was unable to take any time off, which is understandable. So, we were both excited to see Armen, as we are a very close family and very touched that he made the journey for just one week. He would be leaving the UK the following Sunday morning.

Late Saturday evening, the nurse came around to do the obligatory observations, and I was told that my blood pressure was very high. They wanted to stick another needle in me to give me more fluids by drip, but I asked if we could wait until after I drank a jug of water to see how the observations looked then. Fortunately they agreed, and I drank that jug of water like there was no tomorrow—anything to avoid another needle. Thank the Lord, the blood pressure came down; also thank the Lord for catheters.

I managed to have a great sleep and was awakened at 4:00 Sunday morning for more observations. Normally, these observations are done so frequently I have never taken them very seriously. Anyway, the machine said that I had a very high temperature—marvelous. Needless to say I could no longer prolong the dreaded, inevitable needle. The nurse came around and took some blood and sent them off for testing.

On Sunday, June 29, I received a couple of early morning visits from the plastic surgery team and the GI team who were monitoring my progress after the operation. They both mentioned that an ultrasound had been booked for me later in the day. That did not seem so bad; it was only an ultrasound and a change of scenery.

Jessica and Nick came in to visit me around 2:00 p.m., and it was great to see them. They certainly lifted my spirits. While they were visiting, unfortunately, the wheelchair came to pick me up for my ultrasound. Jill, one of the nurses, accompanied me; she was a lovely Irish nurse with a great sense of humor. We arrived at the scanning department and needless to say, it was absolutely dead on a Sunday afternoon with only two radiologists, a bit spooky. Anyway, the doctor did the ultrasound and the next minute I noticed she whipped out a needle. Are you kidding me! She gave me a local anesthetic in my groin and then another for a biopsy where, apparently, blood was coagulating within the mesh. She was unable to get any blood, which was a great sign; this meant that the blood would be dissolved within the bloodstream with the help of antibiotics. The two drains in my neck were taken out, and I got a couple of nice neat stitches on the side, something similar to Dracula bites! It was a relief to get rid of the drips as they were annoying at night, trying to put my head on the side. Sometimes you felt as if you were going to accidentally strangle yourself in your sleep if you turned your head too quickly and the drips would be pulled out.

Sunday night observations were all over the place. A new cannula was put in, and I woke up the next morning with a splitting headache and totally out of it. I saw Dr. Rasheed in the early morning while I went walking for the first time with the physiotherapist; in fact, I think I took the physio for a walk and not the other way around. I had taken myself off the constant oxycodone drip and was only administering as and when I needed it by pushing a button and self-medicating. I saw the plastics team in the early morning as well and felt really embarrassed as I cried in front of them, something I never do. I was at the moment feeling really down with a fair bit of pain from the groin injections and really frustrated with being in hospital, feeling vulnerable. Sometimes, I think it is a good thing to let all your emotions out. I think it is more frustration than anything. New antibiotics were prescribed as well as an inflammatory today, so I was not happy with having to take even more medication. I just need a good night sleep, and my guardian angels can do their work while I am resting.

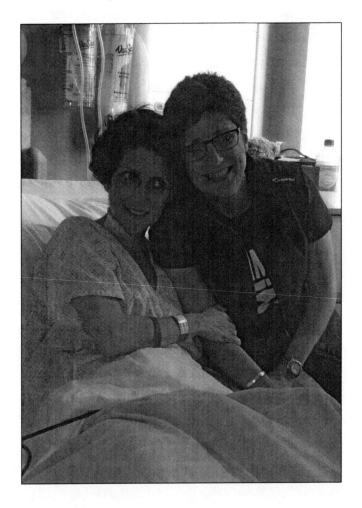

On Monday, I had a really great day. Armen arrived and visited me in the afternoon; it was lovely seeing him looking so well. Armen vegetated in front of my TV monitor watching Wimbledon, while I dozed off, so we were both well sorted. Emil arrived after work, and it was the first time he saw his brother, so it was a lovely reunion.

Early Tuesday morning, John, one of the plastics doctors, arrived at 7:00 and dropped off a lovely cup of coffee for me, which he took from the private patients' lounge. I had mentioned previously how my one vice in life was coffee. Before my cancer scenario kicked off last year, I used to have ten cups of coffee a day and admittedly did not drink enough water. However, since my cancer I have enjoyed a lovely double shot of caffeine in the morning, and that was it for the day. Unfortunately hospital coffee is not the greatest, so I have been skipping coffee in favor of tea. It's not the same but better than nothing. Anyway, Dr. John took my comments on board and dropped off the coffee, what a lovely man. I think he was also feeling sorry for me about my crying episode of yesterday—embarrassing.

The doctors requested that my catheter be taken out along with my morphine drip and one of the two drains in the side of my abdomen. I was relieved to see that things were moving in the right direction. The nurse came around to take one of the drains out, and it was one of the weirdest sensations I have ever felt. I had forgotten, fortunately, how it felt at CUH last year. The senior nurse asked if I would mind if one of the trainee nurses could take out the one drain; of course I am always happy when the youngsters learn and had no qualms about it. Chloe, the trainee nurse, was lovely. She started pulling out the drain, and it was the long one, the only way I can describe the feeling is like a sensation of mice running in your insides the width of your tummy and then popping out. The other drain was pulled out the following day; it was much shorter, thank goodness, but Chloe had to really pull on the end bit to get it out—weird. It was like a bottle of champagne that she was trying to cork.

Later in the morning I went for a shower and the cannula they had put in my hand was annoying me so I asked one of the nurses if they could cover it with a waterproof plaster just in case I needed it later on. Worst case was if I had to have another one put in, and I wanted to avoid a needle scenario at all costs. Well, as it would happen, I was busy drying myself off after a lovely hot shower and all of a sudden I noticed a lot of blood all over the bathroom floor. For the life of me I could not think where it was coming from. Oh well, the cannula that I was trying to preserve so diligently had other ideas. It popped out of my hand, and I immediately put the lovely white towel the nurses gave me for showering onto the opening wound and hoped the bleeding would stop. I also managed to press the emergency alarm button in the bathroom to alert nurses. I opened the bathroom door in my birthday suit, no stoma bag, and really just trying to stem the flow of blood. Four nurses had rushed to the door and saw my predicament, very embarrassing. They taped the opening in my hand with tape, and I could finish my toiletries. I told you I had left my dignity at the door long ago. Needless to say, I spent the next half hour cleaning up the bathroom from all traces of blood; do not ask me how blood even managed to get on the wall and shower curtain.

Three of my work colleagues popped in to visit me in the afternoon, and we made full use of the patients' lounge. It was great seeing them and having a good chuckle. I went to bed tired but very happy that night.

On Wednesday, July 2, Dr. John brought me another coffee at 7:30 in the morning, lovely and very thoughtful of him. The plastics team came to see me at 8:00 and seemed really pleased with my progress. I also managed to walk the two flights of stairs twice over, once in the morning and once in the evening. I am now starting to get mobile and desperately trying to get back my strength. I have been desperate to get around once all my drains were taken out and, thank Jesus, I am able to do this. My good friend, Anne, came to see me and it was lovely to catch up with her and just speak about things unrelated to my illness. Armen, Emil's brother, went to Wimbledon today so I did not see him at all, but Emil came and visited me in the evening after work. I love it when I see him with a big smile on his dial. Every day he sees improvements in me, and that is very encouraging. Dr. Rasheed came around the ward at 6:30 p.m. and seemed really pleased with my progress, even though there was bruising where they injected my groin. It still feels solid as a brick. I ordered for dinner a sandwich and tomato soup and was really looking forward to a nice hot soup. However, the wheel on the trolley near my bed fell off on one corner and the tomato soup flew everywhere—how embarrassing. The catering staff got me more soup, which was very kind of them. It seems that if anything untoward went wrong on the ward, it would happen to me, and I am just having a little giggle about it. My main aim is for the nurses on the ward to not forget me too soon—I am only joking.

On Thursday, July 3, I decided to go for an early morning shower. I was caught on the hop; while I was blow-drying my hair, the plastics team arrived. Oh well, a girl has to keep her standards while in hospital. I have to say that whenever I have stayed in a hospital, I have always tried to get my morning showers in as soon as possible. It just makes you feel a lot better and boosts your morale. Don't worry; I stop at putting on a full face of makeup in the hospital. A shower is enough for me.

I mentioned to the plastics team that I was experiencing a lot pain in my tummy, and that my stoma had doubled in size. I had only realized this in the shower. It was ridiculous, but a grown woman getting upset about not pooing. I just felt frustrated that I had, by God's grace, got so far and done so well, and then a minor issue like pooh was distressing me—ridiculous. They prescribed me some laxido, lactulose, and a suppository to be put in my stoma. Well, the nurse came to administer the suppository and as she pushed it, it decided it wanted out. I was then asked to lie down for ten minutes and press the suppository down for that duration of time—very embarrassing but I was so desperate for this constipation to remedy itself, I would have done anything. All morning, nothing happened and I was getting desperate as I was supposed to be discharged the next day. Armen came to visit me and we went out for a walk down Fulham Road and had a lovely ice coffee and cake to share. I was so uncomfortable that it was the last thing I wanted to do, but I was conscious that I needed the exercise and it was good to get out in such beautiful sunshine. I did not eat dinner that evening as I was so uncomfortable and felt so bloated. If anybody says they have had constipation, I will definitely sympathize with them. It is really painful, and you can hardly breathe or walk from how uncomfortable you feel.

On Friday, July 4, at 3:20 a.m., I got up and walked the stairs in Marsden. It was a lovely time fellowshipping with the Lord Jesus at that time of the morning with no one around. Don't get me wrong; I was crying and praying earnestly to my Father in Heaven, discussing so many things that were happening in my life and the sights I was seeing in the ward. Psychologically, being in the ward for a long period of time, you notice how evil the curse of cancer is and how the devil is operating.

People need to know the love of Jesus. He is a good God, and all good things come from Him. Illness and disease are not from our Lord; we were not created for illness but for prosperity, freedom, and blessing. The Garden of Eden was perfect; everything we ever required, needed, and wanted was there for our enjoyment. Unfortunately, the sly devil, who has no authority, duped Eve, and this is how we saw sin and sickness enter the earth. This was not what God intended for his people, and I was getting really distressed and angry. I was getting emotionally attached to the ladies and helping them out whenever I could. Most of them were in their 80s and 90s. They were really stoic and an amazing example of resilience. I talked to them about the Lord Jesus Christ. A lot of them loved the Lord, and that was great to know.

I had not had any morphine for two and a half days now and thank the Lord for that. Fentanyl and oxycodone had made me so constipated, so now I was just on paracetamol and antibiotics. Dr. John came around at 7:30 a.m. with another cup of coffee for me, and we had a nice early morning chat. He was very sympathetic with my pooh situation—I call it "Pooh Gate." He mentioned that the plastics and GI teams would be visiting me later. The teams came around and neither were too concerned about me. They mentioned that it might be trapped wind and constipation and also fluid on the tummy wall, which can be sorted out with more antibiotics. They did mention that they would book a CT scan that morning for me, which was reassuring but really annoying. You know what this means—another cannula. At this stage I did not care; I was so uncomfortable.

At 10:00, the ward nurse came to do the cannula; it looked massive. Anyway, she kindly gave me some Ametop cream to numb the area where she was planning on stabbing me, which did help. Sometimes I think I am such a drama queen, but at this stage I was feeling and looking like a pin cushion. The other reason for this was that every night, the nurse used to come around and give each patient an injection to avoid blood coagulating. My thighs were black and blue, but it was needed, so no arguing. Also, those very fetching white stockings also help to prevent deep vein thrombosis (DVT); I did not mind them as they kept me warm at nights, and they prevented hair growth—sorry, but it is true.

At 11:00 a.m., a porter with a wheelchair arrived to take me up for the CT scan. I was grateful that it was so quick, and things were getting done. At 6:00 p.m. the GI Team came around and told me that the CT scan showed nothing untoward. There was a large build-up of pooh and dried blood that antibiotics would clear—thank you, Lord. Soon after they left, the nurse came around with an enema. Well, I have to say I had never experienced this before, and I was not too sure what to expect. I don't mean to sound as if I have an obsession with pooh but to be honest, after this episode I think I do. Apologies to the readers for too much information I am about to give.

Anyway, the nurse applied some gel to my stoma and proceeded to push into my stoma the enema full of liquid. Well, the next minute, a chocolate fountain exploded out of my small little stoma—who would have known. Thank goodness, the nurse had the sense to put a large towel over me and the bed. It was like a blocked drain that needed a rod stuck down to get rid of all the muck. Needless to say, I had a shower after this episode and started feeling a bit more normal and breathing a lot easier. The nurse came back to my bed after my shower and applied new dressings to my wounds. I did not realize that Dr. Rasheed was outside my curtain, waiting for us to finish; this was around 7:40 on a Friday evening—the poor surgeon works all hours. Dr. Rasheed and I had a lovely chat, and I was sorry to see him for the last time. I gave him a big hug and thanked him for everything. I mentioned what an amazing helper he has been to my Maker. Dr. Rasheed is truly blessed with a God-given talent, and he is saving lives— what a gift from above. He is such a genuinely humble guy with a wicked sense of humor—amazing.

All night I pooh'd until I could pooh no more—thank you, Jesus—what a relief. Small things like this mean so much to patients and are a sign of getting well. I was so excited I just wanted to do cartwheels down the ward.

On Saturday, July 5, a nurse came around with more Laxido and paracetamol. I think I have had enough Laxido aka "pooh destroyers" for the moment. I had a meeting with the plastics and GI teams, and all seemed pleased with my progress. Around midmorning, the ward nurse came around and asked if I would mind if I was moved to the ward next door for my last night as they had a patient from ICU coming down for a long stay. The ward next door was for short stays. Of course, I did not mind, in fact it was the ward I was in around five weeks prior, and I preferred it as it was not a thoroughfare. I had a nice corner bed stuck away and nobody passing—lovely.

Emil and Armen came around 3:00 p.m. and took me out to the coffee shop in Fulham Road I had previously visited on Thursday. It was a lovely walk, and I shared a delicious chocolate ganache slice with Emil. We got back to the ward, and I was keen for Emil and Armen to leave around 5:00 as it was Armen's last night in London, and I wanted them to enjoy each other's company. I was very sad to see Armen leave but also very grateful for the time he was with us. Armen is the biggest tennis fan in the world, and he was absolutely crestfallen that he would be on the flight back to L.A. while the men's single finals were played between Federer and Djokovic.

On Saturday night, sleep was very hard to come by. There were only two of us in the short-stay ward and Jean, the eighty-four-year-old lady, was going through the wars.

Earlier on in the day she was violently ill a couple of times, and the nurses had to put a tube down her nose to her tummy, which is most uncomfortable, and I could sympathize with her. They then could not find a vein to put drips in and tried three times. My heart really felt for her, and I was really emotionally affected by this. I had to leave the ward while the nurses were there and went for a walk up and down the stairs just praying to Jesus to help Jean. I was angry with God; I know full well it is not God's doing, but all I could see was the suffering around me and the struggles poor Jean was going through, though I knew that this was not what God intended for us. I was so emotional I could not stop crying. A couple of the nurses saw the state I was in, and I witnessed to them and they knew where I was coming from.

I have the highest admiration for doctors and nurses who are so stretched in their jobs and yet so accommodating to all patients. The nurses did mention to me that the way they cope with patients coming in and out so frequently was not to get too up close and personal with them. For me that is difficult to do; as soon as I meet someone they kind of become my friend. It must be so difficult to look after someone, sometimes intimately, and then treat them with courtesy and respect and then send them on their way, and wait for the next patient to arrive—amazing!

That Saturday night, I did not sleep well at all. Poor Jean was poorly and her monitors were beeping most of the night. Jean and I were the only ladies in the ward, so we got up at around 6:00 in the morning, and I fetched Jean a cup of tea and I had my cup of coffee. I had a shower and then prepared myself for my imminent departure. The GI team came around 9:00 and gave me one last thorough look over before I left. They seemed really happy with everything, and, thank the Lord, my stoma was behaving itself perfectly. One of the lovely nurses changed my dressing where my drains were and left the big scar from my belly button to pubic bone free of dressings. The scar was drying out nicely; just the deep little drains were taking a little more time to heal. What was amazing was that the stitches were not staples like the first operation but were disintegrating stitches inside, with glue on the outside.

I packed all my greeting cards away and left the couple of colorful helium balloons with Jean for her to enjoy for her duration in the ward. Emil came to pick me up at 10:30 a.m., and it was lovely to finally be going home. I went around the whole ward and kissed all the ladies goodbye. I was really quite emotional and was going to miss each one of them, even Margaret who was eighty-three years old and who was deaf and dumb. I took her under my wing when I was lying in bed opposite her, and I used to select her food for her, put her TV on, gave her my dressing gown to keep warm. She had her own personality and was rather stubborn when she wanted to be, but I was very fond of her. I was really sad to say goodbye to the lovely nurses on Ellis Ward. It was nice to hear them say that I was a pleasure to look after, and they will miss me. I think I will miss them more. I find, when leaving the hospital after an extended period, I get nervous about my aftercare, but that is normal I guess.

Emil was waiting in the reception area of the Royal Marsden and had booked a taxi home; fortunately we only had to wait five minutes before it arrived. It was about a forty-minute trip to Croydon on Sunday; traffic was light, and I could not wait to get home, albeit rented. Bless Emil; he had made an amazing yellow split pea soup for me, which I relished for the next couple of days. The doctor's did say that I would need to eat soft foods for the first couple of weeks—nothing too harsh like brown foods, fruits, and vegetables.

I cannot tell you how excited I was to be home. I know it is wrong of me, but every time I go into hospital I always wonder whether I would ever see my familiar surroundings again. Don't get me wrong; I long for the day to go home to my Lord Jesus Christ who has a mansion prepared for me in heaven, but it is wonderful seeing Emil and family again. Thank the Lord, most of my family are believers in Christ, and I have an amazing network of family and friends who continually pray for me and enfold me with their love.

Chapter Thirteen

Life at Home Part 3

*M*onday, July 7, was pretty uneventful, and I felt a bit sore and decided to stay indoors and get onto my laptop and watch some God TV. I so missed my spiritual food while I was in the hospital. I did of course take my Bible with me and read one of Andrew Wommack's books, but I just love watching Christian TV, my favorite ministers; passion for Christ, and the scriptural teachings they share. Monday was also a good day as we have finally heard from our lawyers that we should be completing on our new flat this Friday, July 11.

On Tuesday I called Ellis Ward just to see how Jean was feeling; she was so much on my mind. The ward nurse mentioned that she was doing well, so I asked her to send Jean my love and let her know I was praying for her.

On Thursday morning, I called my doctor's office early and asked for an emergency appointment. The dressing on my drain incisions was leaking, and I needed a new prescription. The pharmacy at the Royal Marsden was closed on Sunday, so they were unable to dispense any drugs for me. However, thank you, Jesus, the only drugs I needed were paracetamol and ibuprofen. I also now required some small dressings to cover my drain holes. So I was fortunate enough to get an appointment at 9:20 that morning, and I saw one of the GP's who kindly changed my dressing and provided me with a prescription. I then walked to the pharmacy to pick up the prescription, and I was feeling so good I decided to pop into the supermarket to do a small bit of shopping. Silly, silly me! I only got one bag of groceries, but when I got home I was in a bit of pain. I had really pushed myself and had strong words with myself for being so silly—I won't do that again. The doctors did tell me that I was not allowed to carry anything over 2.2lbs within the first six weeks of surgery—ouch!

In the midmorning on Friday, July 11, we heard that we had closed on our flat—thank you, Jesus. It has been such a long time coming—about seventeen months since negotiations started. Emil was keen to close on the eleventh as it was exactly a year to the date when this evil cancer episode kicked off in my life. I am just so excited that we have finally closed, and now we can start moving some of our stuff out of the rental flat to ours—I am of course supervising the whole process. Tomorrow we have a delivery of some new furniture arriving, so God's timing has been perfect. On Saturday, July 19, all our furniture from storage arrives back and on the twenty-first, the decorators and my brother-in-law, the landscape gardener, will start their work and should all be finished by Friday, July25. Emil's birthday is on Saturday, July 26, so we are arranging a big family get together, along with some close friends for a birthday/house warming party—can't wait.

Wednesday, July 23, I had a clinic appointment at the Royal Marsden in Chelsea with Dr. Rasheed. The day before, I had baked a big cake for the nurses in Ellis Ward and another cake for Dr. Rasheed and his team to enjoy when I see them. I arrived at Ellis Ward early on Wednesday and dropped off the cake and had a lovely chat to a few of the nurses on duty. It was lovely to catch up with them all and jokingly asked if I could be readmitted as I missed them all so much. I am so indebted to them all for nursing me so well and always with a smile on their faces. Nursing is definitely a calling you have to have in order to cope with the stresses of day-to-day life in the wards, and all kudos to them.

I then went down to clinic and waited for my 3:00 p.m. appointment. Unfortunately, clinic was running an hour late so I finally got to see Dr. Rasheed at 4:00 p.m. It is unbelievable to see the amount of cancer patients going through the clinic doors, each one of them a very sad story I am sure. Thank God I have the joy of the Lord as my strength and His peace flowing through me every time I go to clinic, as it is heart breaking some of the sights, especially the children affected by this curse of cancer.

I gave Dr. Rasheed a big hug, and it was lovely to have a good laugh with him. He has an amazing sense of humor, and we just bounce off each other. We ran through a few things, and Dr. Rasheed looked at my scar and felt the mesh in my tummy and seemed really pleased with my progress. In fact, he could not believe how well I was looking. I did ask him if I would need more chemo or radiotherapy, and he said that I would need both or one or the other. At that moment I rebuked what he was saying in my mind. I also asked about my stoma reversal, if he could do it as I trusted him and enjoyed the Marsden. He said that if the stoma could be reversed then he would be the one that would definitely do the reversal as it will be complicated if it can be done. Of course it can be done; I know that my Lord God is able. Jesus did not create me with a stoma, so this is going to be reversed in His holy name.

Okay, so the other "thing" I asked Dr. Rasheed about was S E X. I apologies for those reading this book about providing TMI (too much information). Dr. Rasheed was very funny and very quick in his response. He asked if I desperate because of the hot weather—I must say it has been hitting the high sixties but no, that was not the reason. I was just curious to know when it would be safe. I have to say, since last July I can count on one hand when my loving husband and I have "done it," and I have to say,

I missed it terribly. The outcome was that I can commence lifting weights and having sex and getting back to normal six weeks after the operation. I gave Dr. Rasheed a big hug when I left, and it was agreed that I would see him on August 15 when, hopefully, he will have the results from the operation by then.

I must say, to be honest, I walked out of the consultation rather deflated and was desperate to go home and get a hug from Emil. Emil had to stay at home in the new flat as he was busy with my brother-in-law on the terrace, and the decorators were inside doing the wallpaper. I would have loved him to come with me, but in a way I needed the alone time to gather my thoughts and pray. I arrived home to a new home full of surprises as all the new curtains were hung, the wallpaper was up, and the new furniture in place; it definitely cheered me up, and we were both looking forward to moving in. Emil's birthday was on the Saturday, July 26, and we wanted to wake up in our new home the morning of the big day.

On Emil's birthday, we did awaken in our new bedroom, and it was lovely. I love the smell of new carpets! I made Emil breakfast in bed, and then we got up early and started preparing for a birthday party/house-warming party with friends and family. Everyone arrived on Saturday at midday, and it was lovely to see everyone in our new place. The weather was absolutely gorgeous so we sat outside on the terrace and enjoyed Emil's Armenian cooking.

On Sunday, July 27, Emil and I went to our lovely church to fellowship and worship with our Christian family. It was amazing to see everyone again, and I was smothered with hugs and kisses from everyone. I just thank the Lord that I was among everyone again worshiping Him, I have missed them terribly. The weather has been unbelievably hot in London the past few weeks, and it was lovely to go after church and stop off for a cold, iced Frappuccino and cake—yummy. I must say, since my operation I have been eating anything I fancied and enjoying myself while doing it. I am not too concerned about putting on weight as I know I will lose it when I start getting active and go to the gym after the six-week curfew.

Wednesday, July 30, I had cleaners come in and do a final cleaning of the rental property before we hand over the keys to the rental property. I had a young Bulgarian lady arrive at 10:00, and she was at the flat for a few hours cleaning. I would have been happy doing the cleaning of the rental myself as Emil and I am both OCD tidy, but our landlord insisted he needed an invoice from a cleaning company. On the thirtieth at 4:00, I had a gentleman arrive at the rental flat to do an inventory check-out and see if everything was in order, and I finally handed over all the rental flat keys—I was relieved and excited to do this, as we finally had just one flat and it was ours. Now, Emil and I can live in our new flat with relative hassle-free lives.

The other great news is that for the past few days I had stopped taking paracetamols in the morning and evenings. I had been feeling stronger by the day and just resting some afternoons for an hour in the afternoon, although it is sometimes a struggle to get to sleep. My scar has been healing well on the top although toward the pubic bone there were some nasty discoloration. However, I am not too concerned about it. Also, when I press the bottom part of my scar, I don't feel much sensation at all. Dr. Rasheed did say that it was where the mesh was and that I would not totally get my feeling back. If that is the only side effect, then thank you, Jesus; I am alive and feeling great and life is good.

At the moment I am typing this book and listening to UCB radio and have the TV on mute. I am looking at some silly home-shopping channel, and they are selling some sort of diet and exercise plan. I just realize how shallow my life was before my illness. I used to be into health, fitness, and looking good for my age. I am not saying it is not important to be healthy, but to spend so much time being self-obsessed with triviality like this is a waste of time. It is similar to those young people who look up to so-called role models in celebrities; they are just normal human beings who are as sinful as the next person but just happened to be in the right place at the right time—most of the time doing the wrong things. This illness has taught me to be focused on the Lord Jesus Christ who is my hope and everlasting future. That is what is important.

On Sunday, August 3, Emil's mother came to visit for three weeks from Los Angeles. It was great to have her, and of course, Emil was in his element. We have unfortunately not been over to see Emil's family for a couple of years now, and it is always lovely to have them over. They are so easy to accommodate and very helpful. She is an amazing homemaker and cook, but I have to be honest, sometimes two women in a kitchen do not always run smoothly. I have been consistently baking cakes and cookies for the various builders and marketing, sales, and concierge people on site. They have all been most helpful to us during our recent move and were always willing to come over at short notice to sort out various issues we may have. We are truly blessed where we are living now and enjoying every moment.

Friday, August 15, my sister's husband, Nick, came over to finish off our roof garden and I have to say it looks lovely. Mom was happy to help out with the planting, and we both found ourselves covered like pigs in mud after a morning of lugging compost, substrata, and bark to the beds. It was thoroughly enjoyable, and I was proud of myself for being able to help out—thank you, Lord.

Emil and I left after lunch on Friday and made our way slowly to the Royal Marsden in Chelsea for my 3:20 appointment. We first stopped off at the Ellis Ward, and I dropped off a tin of home-baked flapjacks for the nurses and had a little chat; it was lovely to see them again. Nothing has changed, they are all still so busy, and the ward is still full of the curse of cancer that prevails in society. Unfortunately, Dr. Rasheed's surgery was an hour late again! Every time I see Dr. Rasheed, he is late, but he also is of course really busy and looks really tired, poor man. Apparently, he had two new cases to see before me, and I can imagine what those poor families they must be going through. I am just so grateful for the blood of Jesus that covers me every time I go to the hospital and the joy of the Lord that is my strength.

We finally saw Dr. Rasheed and handed over the obligatory tin of home baked goodies for him and his team. He was in good spirits and joking as ever. He did mention that he felt sorry for Emil after our last meeting, and he wanted to call Emil up and warn him about my supposed sex drive—alright, so I said it, and it seemed funny at the time. After our initial joking around, he got serious and said that he was disappointed with the results from my surgery. He mentioned that they had shaved off as much pubic bone as they possibly could and wanted to preserve the bladder due to my age and lifestyle and did not want to give me another bag—I totally agreed. He said that the results showed that there were still small malignant tumor cells around the pubic bone and bladder wall areas where they had cut, and that he believed that radiotherapy was the

way forward. I smiled and thanked Jesus there and then—
no more chemo! Isn't the Lord Jesus Christ amazing? I had
been praying that I would not need any more chemo as I
hated the whole IV scenario; I was absolutely dreading it,
and God in his mercy gave me another miracle.

After I hugged Dr. Rasheed, followed by booking
another visit with him for a mid-November time, we
left. I was buzzing, knowing that I would not have to do
any more chemo, but on the other hand upset that the
tumors had not gone altogether. Dr. Rasheed mentioned
that at this stage, they did not know if they would develop
and grow or not but believed radiotherapy would eradi-
cate them.

I of course rebuked straight away all the negative news
I was hearing, and my trust is in the Great Physician, who
made me and formed me before time even began, who
knows my name, and who died for me—He is the one I
put my trust in and know full well I am healed in His time
and to His glory.

So many times people ask, "Why do Christians, if we
are so blessed and loved by God, go through trials?" My
answer is "Why not?" Satan is like a roaring lion seeking
those he can destroy, and all sickness and diseases are
from Satan. As a child of God, I know that I have authority
and power over Satan through the cross of Jesus Christ.
At the cross is where it all begins and ends for Christians.
We are saved, sanctified, and redeemed at the cross, and

we are given everlasting life through the raising of Jesus at the cross. Jesus died for me and rose again for me to intercede and talk to God on my behalf. He is interceding for me up in heaven right now, and I am blown away by His love and mercy for me, a sinner, who does not deserve His mercy and grace—thank you, Jesus.

So, although I was feeling a bit down, I have to be honest. I just had to pick up my Bible and read all His promises and benefits and trust in the Lord for full healing so that His name may be glorified and that friends, colleagues, and family may come to know the Lord Jesus Christ as their personal friend and savior and lover of their souls.

On Monday, August 18, I arrived at the Royal Marsden in Sutton for my 2:45 p.m. appointment, knowing already what was likely to be said. Okay, so now I know that the devil is toying with me, and I thank the Lord for his infinite peace that he is providing me. Unfortunately, I heard that I would have to go through chemo and radiotherapy at the same time for a probable duration of six weeks solid. The great news is that I will only be taking the chemo tablets and not have to go through the horrible IV. So, I am totally blessed and grateful for these small mercies that I am continually receiving, although I would prefer no chemo whatsoever.

It was lovely to see Ramani in the meeting with the doctor as it seems a lifetime away since I saw her last.

She is the amazing clinical nurse stationed at the Royal Marsden in Sutton who has been such an amazing help to me in the past. She mentioned that, for those people in the know, my TNM numbers were; T4, N2 and M1. To be honest, I have always believed that ignorance is bliss, but for reasons of this book I asked her to explain, although I am not sure I understand anyway. T4 means Tumors 4 (Stage 4 cancer). N2 means Lymph Nodes 2 and M1 means Metastases 1. I am presuming 2 and 1 are low figures, and that it is pretty good. I definitely do not dwell on what the doctors and nurses say, and I don't believe cancer patients should wholly believe their reports, either. As believing Christians, we need to focus on our Maker, the Great Physician, who knows all things and rebuke all negative information that comes our way. I do not believe Christians are burying their heads in the sand, like some people believe we are. I know and trust that my God is able, and I put my hope and trust in Him alone.

I received a letter in the mail, requesting a meeting at the Royal Marsden in Sutton with Dr. Tait on the Tuesday, September 2. I know that Dr. Tait is the lady who will be responsible for the radiotherapy. Her team will also be tattooing me with markers where the lasers are to be placed during radiotherapy. Thank goodness, things are moving pretty fast, and there will not be too much hanging around, waiting for something to happen.

Chapter Fourteen

Chemotherapy and Radiotherapy

I arrived at the Royal Marsden in Sutton for my 2:30 p.m. appointment, and thank goodness I did not have to wait too long. I was shown into the waiting room and saw one of Dr. Tait's team who ran through my next steps and the side effects of pelvic radiotherapy.

I did mention to her that I would rather not hear and just let's do it. All throughout my illness I have always had the mindset that you have to go through what you are going through for a reason, so what is the point of hearing side effects that may or may not affect you? If they do, then fine; we'll deal with it. The less you know the better you are placed in not imagining and exaggerating symptoms that were told to you in the appointments. You let your own body tell you what it is feeling and if, indeed, it is a symptom of what you are going through. Ignorance is bliss, and I totally believe it. Whenever I leave the clinical appointments, so often they are negative and worst-case scenarios, I rebuke whatever has been said in the meeting and trust the Lord Jesus to pull me through.

Ramani then popped into the room and provided me with a whole lot of data and booklets on pelvic radiotherapy, preparing your bladder for CT scan, side effects of Capecitabine chemo with radiotherapy, and so forth. I glanced at the common side effects, and there was a list as long as my arm. I am rebuking all side effects right now as they are not going to harm me in any way.

The one thing that is worrying me is that every day of the radiotherapy treatment I have to fill my bladder with 700 mls of water and then wait for one hour before I have the radio. Apparently the bladder has to be comfortably full. Well, I just hope I can keep my bladder comfortably full and not have an accident on the radiotherapy table. I do struggle with not going to the loo for long periods of time and especially after drinking so much water. Oh well, we will see. I might have to practice at home, keeping water inside me for an hour before I go for my CT scan and radiotherapy.

Before leaving the Marsden, I was given my appointment card to say that the CT scan would take place on Friday, September 5, where they would tattoo markings where the radiotherapy would be targeted. On September 15, I had an appointment to go to the chemo clinic and hopefully I could then commence the six weeks of chemo and radiotherapy. Before all this happened, the doctor did mention that they wanted to have an MRI scan done of my pelvis before the treatment commenced, so I am now waiting for a letter from the hospital with the MRI scan date. I cannot wait to commence the treatment and get back to work as soon as possible.

Talking about work, my employer has been amazing. God has been merciful and blessed us abundantly. I am still being paid, and I cannot tell you how grateful we both are for this. Unfortunately, when cancer strikes anyone, you do not realize how expensive it can be, paying for extra heating bills, travel fares, parking, and so on. Thank the Lord we do not have these worries with my salary being paid, but I feel desperately sorry for those cancer sufferers not in such a fortunate, blessed position as me.

I arrived early in the morning of Friday, September 5, and fortunately the radiotherapy team were able to see me half hour early, which was a miracle. I had a lovely nurse put the dreaded cannula in my arm, and I mentioned to her the stress I was feeling about drinking so much water and then having to wait an hour before going for the CT scan. She was kind enough to recommend that I only drink two glasses of water and go into the scan a half hour afterward, which was a huge relief for me. Funny enough, all throughout my cancer, I have not stressed so much as retaining the water I thought I had to—thank you,

Jesus. The nurse also mentioned that whatever I do today will be the same for the six weeks of radiotherapy, which I did not realize. So drinking only two glasses of water and waiting half an hour is a huge help for me.

After the half hour, I was taken through to have the CT scan. I was provided with one of those sexy hospital gowns and told to come through when I was ready. Well, I have never felt so much like a beached whale as when I lay on the CT scanning table. Usually I am okay to shift myself up and down and make myself comfortable. This time around, because the nurses were placing the markers on my pelvis where they were going to tattoo, I was told to lay still with dead weight, and they would move me. Thank goodness I had shaved my legs and got my nice Wolford knickers on! You just never know when these things are required, and moms are so right: you have to wear "clean" underwear as you never know when you might be run over by a bus or something.

I lay on the table being moved around and given the dye where the contrast could be seen on the x-rays. The nurse then came through and marked a spot with an x on my left and right side of my hip bone and a mark near my belly button. She then did a tiny pin prick in the middle of each x and placed ink as a permanent marker. It was not painful, but I could not imagine doing a whole arm, back, or leg with pin pricks and getting tattoos put all over my body. It must be painful after a while, and I must say, being of an older generation, they don't look very nice. I have always associated tattoos with sailors, so I am always amazed to see beautiful young ladies with lovely feminine dresses on and they turn around with big black tattoos on their backs, shoulders, legs, or arms. Why?

After the CT scan was over, the nurses gave me my hospital appointment card with all six weeks of daily radiotherapy appointment times put inside. It looks like I start the course of radiotherapy on September 17. I am due to see the chemo clinic on Monday, September 15, so they will probably provide me with chemo tablets then for the duration of the six weeks. Next week, on Wednesday, the tenth, I am due to visit the plastics team in Chelsea Marsden, which will be nice to catch up with them. On Thursday, September 11, I am scheduled for an MRI scan in Sutton Marsden, so things are definitely moving quickly.

I have also been told that every Tuesday, I have to visit the chemo clinic to check on my liver enzymes, blood platelets, and so forth to monitor and see if it is good for me to continue with the tablets. On Thursdays I have to visit the radio clinic to check that everything is going fine with no burns on skin, no irritations, and so on, so I am rebuking all negative things that might hinder my progress and ultimate healing. In Jesus' name, I am going to sail through the next six weeks with A+ gold stars and give my Creator all the glory and honor due to Him.

On Wednesday, September 10, I went for an early morning appointment up to the Marsden in Chelsea. I seem to call it the Marsden Hotel instead of Hospital for some odd reason, but then again, I had such an amazing time while I was in and so well looked after, it did sometimes feel like a hotel. Fortunately, I saw Dr. Ramsey, the plastic surgeon, on time, and it was lovely catching up with him. When he first came into the room I did say that "I hope he recognized me with my clothes on." It was nice seeing him again, but every time I have seen him in the past it was in a hospital gown. Thank goodness, he caught the joke. I really need to make a mental note to stop joking so much as some people might not catch the joke, and I may land in trouble. Dr. Ramsey prodded my tummy and seemed pleased with my progress. He did mention that I would not have much sensation around my pubic bone and lower tummy for at least eighteen months. After that period of time, I will then be able to determine what feeling will be left for the rest of my life. It is a very odd sensation when I press my lower tummy and I cannot feel anything; it just feels like sponge. He did say that it was the mesh he put in my tummy but some of it is degradable so I just have to wait and see after eighteen months what sensations I am left with. I had baked a load of shortbread, and I left a large container for Dr. Ramsey and his team to enjoy over a cup of tea.

I arrived back home around lunch time and lay down; I am finding myself tiring a lot quicker these days, but I put it down to eating a load of food and not exercising too much. Around 3:00 in the afternoon I got a call from the plastics team in Chelsea. Whenever I get a call from the hospital, I start thinking the worst, which is not the right thing to do, I know. Anyway, it was a lovely lady and her colleague on the phone to thank me for the lovely shortbread I had baked and to tell me how delicious it was. I was really touched by that telephone call; it is not often people bother these days being so polite and kind. I thanked them for all the amazing work they were doing and promised I would bake some more goodies when I saw the clinic again.

On Thursday, September 11, I went to the Marsden in Sutton for a scheduled 5:00 p.m. MRI Scan. I arrived a half hour early and fortunately they could see me as the previous appointment did not show up—thank you, Jesus. I put on the very fetching RMH hospital gown and went through to the theater. I recognized one of the previous ladies from the last scan, and we had a nice catch up chat. Of course, it is not often you can go to the hospital without a needle somewhere. I did ask the nurse to pinch me hard when she gave me the injection as it seems to ease the feeling somewhat. I received the contrast injection in my upper arm and lay down for thirty minutes while the MRI machine made a big noise. Fortunately, I was able to lie still for the duration of the scan after the nurses had put some sponges underneath the scanning sheet on my pelvis. I left a half hour earlier than expected, which was a bonus and managed to catch the bus and train back home.

On Friday, September 12, around lunchtime I received a call from the Marsden in Sutton. It was Dr. Tait's team. The doctor on the line mentioned that my start date for radiotherapy had been pushed back from September 17 to September 23; this was due to the team trying to work out the best radiotherapy treatment for me. She mentioned that they were working on the protons and neutrons and which was the best way forward. To be honest with you, I switch off after the doctors get too technical, and I would rather not know the intricacies. I have always maintained that ignorance is bliss, and I stand by that 100 percent. No matter what you find out, you still have to go through what the doctors are recommending, so there is absolutely no reason for me to know any more than the start and finish dates of different treatments, which is the only thing that interests me. I am always amazed by patients who look up on the Internet similar cases to what they have and what was prescribed, what to avoid, and so forth. All I know is that I have Jesus Christ on my side, carrying me through this ordeal and knowing that at the end of this, I will have one amazing testimony to God's honor and glory.

I also am quite adamant that no one takes me to and from the hospital anymore. It was great having my sister with me initially, and she was a great help when I was going through my chemo. She started a new job after the fourth cycle, and then Emil took me for chemotherapy IVs. Now, with all my clinic and scan appointments, I go myself and will also go to radiotherapy daily on my own. The curse of cancer that the devil has put in me has taken up far too much valuable time of mine and for the loved ones around me. In fact, I am getting to a point where I am getting really annoyed and pissed off with the devil for messing with a child of God's like this—how dare he. This cancer is one big inconvenience, and I have wasted far too much effort and time on it. But, I know that through this illness, so many people have been inspired and are now questioning their faith, which is great. I have done a few small sermons at my church and, in fact, last Sunday we had a visitor to our church who had just been diagnosed with cancer. He was touched by my testimony and sermon of God's mercies, and I thank Jesus for that. More and more I am praying that the Lord Jesus Christ use me as an instrument for the furtherance of the gospel. Do you know that gospel means good news? The good news of Jesus is what so many people in this day and age are looking for. Well, it is free and available to all who seek the Lord Jesus; it does not cost a thing!

On Monday, September 15, I announced my arrival at the reception only to be told that I needed to take the two blood forms and go give blood—again. I have to say, cancer patients have to relinquish a lot of blood whether they like it or not and by this time, usually, you are so bruised, you start looking like a drug addict. After giving blood, I then went to the chemo clinic to see Professor Cunningham and his team. I got to see a lovely young lady doctor who ran through the chemo tablets and what to expect; funny enough, I knew all about it as I had been on the exact same tablets before. In my mind, I rebuked all negative side effects straight away (diarrhea, blood clots, soreness and redness of hands and feet, mouth ulcers, nausea and vomiting, tiredness and lethargy, and taste changes).

The great news is that instead of six weeks of radio and chemo they had dropped it to four weeks; however, they are going to up the dosage of tablets. During the last chemo cycle, I had five capecitabine tablets a day (3 tablets in the morning and 2 tablets in the evening). This time around, I have to take four tablets in the morning and three tablets in the evening. To be honest, I prefer the short sharp course of action; get it over and done with and God willing, return back to work as soon as possible. I am still praying I go back to work in the first week of November.

I also got to see the lovely Ramani, my clinical worker, with the doctor and gave her a tin full of shortbread I had baked for her and her team. I like spoiling hospital staff as I always feel, especially in cancer hospitals, most of the patients are so drugged up and "out of it" that they do tend to forget the hospital staff who are looking after them. I totally understand, but while I have my marbles about me, I intend to bake goodies whenever I go in for clinic visits.

After leaving the doctor and Ramani, they provided me with a prescription for the chemo tablets I had to drop off at the Pharmacy in the hospital. When I arrived at the pharmacy, there was an hour wait—please, Lord, give me patience. I dropped off my prescription and went to the café and had a sandwich and bottle of water and while I was stuffing my face who should come up to me, my favorite doctor from Aleppo who I used to see when I had my chemo IV earlier in the year in the MDU. It was so nice to see him and I was touched that he recognized me, especially with my very short hair (I had just cut my hair before starting treatment, as I could not be bothered with blow drying). He mentioned that he heard that I had being going through the wars, which I thought was nice he was keeping up to speed on my case, although I am sure, he did not need to. We hugged each other and said our farewells. I then went back to the pharmacy to pick up my tablets after an hour, only to be told that I had not signed a consent form and that I needed to go to the clinic to get the form signed—uuuggghhhhhh! Needless to say, I took a deep breath and went to the clinic to get the consent form signed. The doctor was very apologetic as she had forgotten to get me to sign it and sent me back to the clinic. A further half-hour wait, and I was finally off home. I have to say, waiting around hospitals is not my cup of tea, and I would highly recommend patients bring a very good book to read with them.

I just managed to catch the bus back into Sutton and then the train from Sutton to West Croydon by the skin of my teeth. It was a very long afternoon, and I got home totally exhausted, but thank God the news was positive and the time shortened. I had gotten an appointment scheduled for my first radiotherapy on Tuesday, September 23, at 10:00 a.m. That morning, I need to start taking the chemo tablets within half hour of finishing breakfast and dinner.

I received a phone call on Thursday to say that my treatment scheduled for the twenty-third was delayed until the next day as there was a delay in some sort of equipment required or something. At that moment in time I switched off and just went with the flow.

On Friday in the late afternoon, I received another call from one of the doctors in the radiotherapy department saying that the clinic want to see me on Monday, September 22. She mentioned it was to discuss my treatment going forward as the latest MRI scan indicated the disease was still present near the pubic bone and bladder wall. To be honest, I had already heard this from Dr. Rasheed in Chelsea Marsden. I asked the doctor if I still needed to be in the clinic on Monday, and she said that Dr. Tait needed to see me to discuss the way forward. She mentioned that the radiotherapy and chemotherapy would be delayed until Thursday, September 25—there is that word again—patience.

It is so frustrating, but I know God has a plan in all this, and the doctors are His instruments. I am in the best hands possible, so this is all happening for a reason. I just wish sometimes I did not receive these types of phone calls just before the weekend as it puts a bit of a damper on things. At the back of my mind I am still concerned why they would want me so soon in the clinic if it was not something more sinister.

On Saturday morning I read a scripture from the Word of God which was so poignant and just for me: Habakkuk 3:17–19: "Though the fig tree does not bud ... there are no grapes on the vines...the olive crop fails ... the fields pro-duce no food ... there are no sheep in the pen and no cattle in the stalls, yet I will rejoice in the Lord ...The Sovereign Lord is my strength ... He enables me to go on."

So many times I read verses from the Bible at exactly the right moment in my life, which lift me up and give me such peace and joy, and I thank the Lord for that. Throughout my illness, I have been constantly reminded, reading the Word of God, how the Bible is full of good news that is so relevant to believers today. Below are a few verses which have helped me rejoicing in all things, no matter what life throws at me:

Philippians 4:4	Rejoice in the Lord always, and again I say rejoice.
John 16:33	in the world ye shall have tribulations, but be of good cheer, I have overcome the world.
John 14:1	let not your heart be troubled.
Psalm 34:1	I will bless the Lord at all times, his praise shall continually be in my mouth.

Of course, there are so many scriptures that speak to my heart about joy and peace in these troubled times. In fact the whole book of Philippians is about the apostle Paul and all that he went through, but yet he was the happiest man in the Bible. Paul had the Lord Jesus Christ at the center of his life, and he served others before himself, only thinking of spreading the gospel to the lost souls. I pray that I may have Paul's attitude, which was the same as Jesus' attitude, serving others and being humble and obedient to God's Word.

So, whatever I hear from the doctors on Monday, I will rejoice in knowing that my life is not my own but I belong to Jesus and all good things are from Him. Amen—so be it.

On Monday, September 22, I went with a bit of a heavy heart to the hospital not knowing why they wanted to see me, the uncertainty has got to be the worst part of the whole cancer scenario. I went to reception and was given the obligatory blood form to take to the lab where they could extract the usual red stuff—more needles, hooray! I waited to see the doctors, and thank goodness I was seen early. I was told that I have three tumors that had rapidly grown between the CT scan and MRI Scans, literally within a week of each other. They want me to go for a PET scan this week to see how rapid the tumors are growing, which means another needle and having radioactive stuff injected inside me. I think, if I can remember from the last PET scan, that is what happens. Apparently the tumors will light up with the radioactive dye and indicate which tumors are active, and they can also see if any tumors have spread.

They are still not sure what course of action they are going to take with me, I realize I was complicated, but not this much. Anyway, for the moment, I will not have any radiotherapy, so it is a shame I have had tattoos put on my pelvis in preparation for this. To be honest, full kudos to the hospital for moving things rapidly so this is a minor vain price for me to pay—I think I need to get out more. Unfortunately, there may be a chance that I would have to do more chemotherapy with IVs. I definitely did not want to hear that, as I absolutely hated the last round of chemo that lasted for roughly eight months. I smiled and thanked the doctor, and now it is waiting for the letter from the RMH to let me know when to come in for the PET scan.

I got home from the hospital and closed the front door and cried my eyes out. Trust me, I am not upset with the news, in fact it was better than I expected. The fact that I may have to go through more horrid IV chemo is not an appealing prospect. For a moment I lost the plot, but know that God has a plan, He never does a half-finished job. So Lord, have your way in my life. May your name be glorified in all this mess. At that moment in time, I didn't see an end to this horrid cancer but was fully aware that this body of mine, wracked with cancer, is only a temporary tent on earth. Once dead, my body is just an empty shell, and my spirit and soul are perfected in heaven. At the back of my mind, it seems like a cop-out I know, but to be in heaven is a wonderful prospect, but very selfish of me. I just cannot imagine no more tears, no more sorrow, and no more pain—heaven is going to be a wonderful place where my body is going to be perfect, as the Lord Jesus Christ made it. So for now, I am at peace and trusting God to have His way in my life. Whatever comes my way, let my life be full of peace and joy and may His light shine through me to the lost souls on earth. I don't want my life on earth to be lived in vain; if someone comes to know the Lord through this illness, then I am satisfied.

Monday, September 29, I had to go to RMH for a PET scan. The appointment was scheduled for 11:55 a.m., and I was not allowed to eat for six hours before the scan. Needless to say I had a lovely double shot of coffee and a cereal bar at 5:30 a.m. as I knew I was going to get hungry later on. To not even have a coffee in the morning did not even enter my mind. I arrived at RMH and unfortunately had to wait seventy-five minutes before being seen—yet again I am trying to learn patience through all the visits to hospitals. It does not get easier, I have to say.

I was taken to a room, a cannula was put in my arm, and the nurse flushed saline through and then injected the radioactive dye into my veins. I then had to lie down for one hour for the dye to take effect. I was then taken through for the scan; the machine looks very similar to a CT and MRI scan machine, but I am sure they are completely different. The scan lasted thirty minutes, and then I was discharged. When I left the hospital, I could have eaten my arm, I was so hungry. I had to run for the bus that took me to Sutton train station. Fortunately, there was a wait for the train to West Croydon so I went to Starbucks and bought my favorite cinnamon swirl—yummy!

On Wednesday, October 1, there was a load of Christians around the world praying and fasting for me. I must say, I was most humbled by my fellow Christian brothers and sisters globally spending time praying for me. I just thank the Lord Jesus Christ that we have this amazing Christian family; no matter where we are in the world, we are serving the same loving God. To think that the same God of Abraham, Isaac, and Jacob is my God is mind blowing. We are certainly part of a royal priesthood, a holy nation, and blessed people with power and authority over *all* things.

Now it is a waiting game to wait for the letter to come in the mail from RMH for me to come to the clinic and see what the doctors' next steps are. Thank God I have the Great Physician on my side, and He knows what the future holds and what the next steps are—none better.

Okay, so I have admitted I am not the most patient of people, but I am trying to rest in God, by His grace, to provide me with just an ounce of patience. I know patience is one of the fruits of the Spirit, but this is definitely one I am struggling with *big* time. I ended up calling the clinic on Thursday, October 9, to see if they had made a decision yet as to what the next steps would be in my treatment. I am not really that interested in the results, as I know God has a plan for my life and whatever will come my way, He is able. However, my main concern is for my employer. I mentioned a while ago that I would have loved to commence work in the first week of November, but what with the delay of everything, I really needed to keep my employer in the loop.

The very helpful secretary in the clinic arranged for one of the doctors to call me back and explain the outcome of the PET scan and the next steps going forward. The great news is, and I give the Lord Jesus Christ all the glory, the three tumors are isolated and the cursed cancer had not spread so Amen to that. They will be commencing radio and chemo on Monday, October 20. However, they were not yet sure if it would be a six-week or a four-week cycle. I am praying it will be the shorter version as I am dreading to have to go to the hospital every day for six weeks and take those dreaded chemo tablets. The doctor also mentioned that for whatever reason the treatment did not work and the tumors were still in situ, then I would have to go through more chemo and IVs—here is this worst-case scenario again. I of course rebuked what she just said as I know my life is in God's hands as well as the treatment, so that once this is all over with and I have the all clear, I can publish this book and I can get on with my normal, boring life. I will never again, so help me God, complain about any aspect of my life moving forward. Every day is a bonus for me and a massive blessing.

I have definitely been through some tough times, but in a most bizarre way, I would not change anything. Through it all, God has been at my side, where I can lean on him when things get tough. I know that Jesus has given me a peace and joy throughout this journey of mine that I am even amazed about. Also, He has given me a capacity to forget about the tough times and just to focus on His amazing grace and mercy every day. Every morning I wake up in bed, and I greet the Lord with a good morning song: "This is the day that the Lord has made, I will rejoice and be glad in Him." I get up and have my beloved double shot of coffee and greet the coming day with excitement, not knowing what the Lord has in store for me. God, you are a good God, an amazing God, a personable God, a God who loves little old me—thank you, Jesus; to you be all honor, glory and praise.

On Friday, October 10, Joy, my sister from Australia came to visit Jessica and me in the UK, and it was lovely to see her. It is absolutely perfect timing as she will be with me during my chemo and radiotherapy treatments.

I received a call on Tuesday, October 14 in the evening from one of Dr. Tait's team members to say that they have decided to administer four weeks of chemo tablets and radiotherapy. I was very pleased as it was only four weeks and not the original six weeks as originally discussed. Although I would prefer not to have any chemo tablets again, I am most grateful for the shorter time span. Every time I take chemo tablets, I am so conscious of administering poison to my body, although good poison I know.

Chapter Fifteen

Radiotherapy

—∽◦⚜◦∾—

*M*y sisters and I went out in the afternoon of Thursday, October 16, and visited lovely Penshurst Place. We arrived home at around 6:00 p.m., and I got a call soon after from the Royal Marsden from another member of Dr. Tait's team. The doctor mentioned that they had decided not to administer the chemo tablets at all and only do the radiotherapy for four weeks. I nearly fell backwards; I found myself repeating the question "No more chemo—are you sure?" I am not too sure why; I should not be doubting my Creator and Sustainer in answering my prayers yet again. Thank you, Jesus, for your mercy and grace in answering my prayers about no more chemo. I was desperate not to have chemo tablets again. I was just so happy I was jumping up and down and singing God's praises, I am so happy, ecstatic in fact. The radiotherapy commences on Monday, October 20, and I am praying most earnestly that that will be the end of the curse from Satan.

Monday, October 20, I arrived well in time for my first radiotherapy appointment and was very happy to hand back my chemo tablets, which are now not needed. I was really excited as I know that this is the last leg to my recovery in Jesus' name. I went down to the basement where the radiotherapy treatment rooms are. I was blown away by how cavernous the basement is at the Marsden in Sutton, and how many different radiotherapy rooms are available. I had to go to the Mullard Suite where all the colorectal and pelvic radiotherapy is administered. There are other suites for other cancers such as breast and prostate cancer. I was really impressed by everything, and yet again, it was another side of the Royal Marsden in Sutton I was not aware existed, and at such a huge scale—thank the Lord for the NHS!

My appointment was for 4:00 p.m., so I was taken into a room and asked a few questions and then the radiographer started mentioning all the possible side effects. I had to stop her and say that I was really not interested in hearing about them as I was not going to get them. I mentioned that I was a Christian and totally believed in the nurses and God's healing on my life, and that I would sail through the radiotherapy. She was a lovely young lady and understood where I was coming from—I hope. She then took me through to the changing room, and I had to get into one of those lovely, sexy hospital gowns. Fortunately I was able to keep my top on and my jewelry and they just needed my bottom half exposed—very fetching—not. Moving forward, for the next four weeks of radiotherapy, I think I will take my long pajama bottoms with me, which will be easier to get on and off and save me changing into those gowns again.

I was then lying down on the table with the radiotherapy equipment above and the two radiographers drawing different lines around my tattoos they had administered earlier for this treatment (my very first and definitely last tattoos ever). The radiographers had kindly laid a piece of paper on me to protect my dignity, while they were marking me up. A couple of doctors arrived and were discussing various options to the treatment. A bit embarrassing, but I believe it was to discuss my scar which runs from above my belly button to the very top of my pubic bone. Unfortunately, the scar from the operation goes a bit off center towards my pubic bone, and that was causing a bit of discussion between everyone. I felt like saying they must feel free to help themselves and don't mind me; I definitely felt like a bit of a spare part. Finally, after about a half hour of discussions and markings on my pelvis, the radiotherapy commenced. Well, to be honest, I am not quite sure when it started and finished, it was incredibly fast. I don't think the radiotherapy was longer than a couple of minutes.

Thank you, Jesus, it was not intrusive or painful at all and very quick. The radiographers did mention that the daily treatments will not be as long as the first one, which is great. The only downside is that I had to travel to the hospital on a daily basis for a two-minute treatment. Oh well, it was a small price to pay for my complete healing. Before they started the radiotherapy I prayed for the radiographers and me, that the Lord would enfold us with His love, peace, and guidance during the treatments.

I got dressed and went back to the reception area to pick up my timetable of treatments for the four weeks of radiotherapy. I then walked down to the station and got the train back home. It was while I was on the train that I noticed that the receptionists had given me a timetable for six weeks of radiotherapy. I will have to go back tomorrow and clarify with them that it is indeed four weeks—what Dr. Tait's team had confirmed a week earlier—please, Jesus, only four weeks. I don't fancy going to RMH every day for any longer than that time frame.

When I arrived back in town I popped into the Boots Pharmacy and purchased a pot of aqueous cream for my pelvis. I do have a load of Palmers Cocoa Butter, but unfortunately it is too heavily fragranced, and not recommended by the radiographers. They recommended aqueous cream to rub onto my pelvis to keep the area from drying out, and that I take warm showers instead of baths (not a problem, as I do anyway). Also, I need to pat my tummy dry instead of rubbing it dry (not too sure what I do, will make a mental note). Oh well, let the fun begin, and thank you, Jesus, for being with me yet again and giving me the strength to carry me through these next treatments.

Tuesday, October 22, my radiotherapy treatment was scheduled for 5:10 p.m.; unfortunately there were delays, and I only got to see the radiographers at 5:45 p.m. I know, patience; it is definitely not my forte, and I am still finding myself struggling with it. I totally understand that the hospital is really busy, and I just need to get over it and move on. Anyway, I mentioned that there might be a mistake on my timetable of treatments as it looks like six weeks instead of the four weeks mentioned. I got it wrong; there are thirty treatments scheduled for Monday through Friday which is equal to four full weeks but six weeks, excluding weekends. I hope you understand what I am saying, it took me a while, but then again I am a bit slow when it comes to mathematics. What a shame, anyway, I now have to do the treatments right up to November 28.

I finally left the hospital around 6:00 p.m. and walked down to the train station to get a train to West Croydon. Unfortunately, there had been gale force winds around the UK today, and as a result there were severe delays on the train timetables. Needless to say, patience again, I had to wait for over an hour and a half to get the next train home. I was just starting to feel really sorry for myself and was about to start a pity party all by myself, when a lovely elderly lady came alongside me on the train platform and started speaking to me about the weather. I don't know how the subject came about, but we found ourselves, fellow spirit-filled, Pentecostal Christians, laughing and enjoying each other's company and just sharing how great the Lord Jesus Christ is and how much we love him. It was wonderful and really lifted my spirits at just the right time. God certainly was watching over me and sent that lady to me to encourage me at the exact moment I needed it. I am just amazed that throughout this illness the Lord has been at my side all the time, next to me, watching over me and making me aware of his love around every corner. He has put the right people at just the right time in my path, and I cannot thank Him enough. Little old me, and the Creator of the Universe is thinking about me—awesome!

Theologically speaking the Lord Jesus Christ is omnipresent (everywhere at all times), omnipotent (all powerful), and omniscient (all knowing). What a mighty God I serve, what an amazing Father who by the spoken Word created and designed all things, Sustainer of everything. I love you Jesus.

Another thing that came in the mail last week was a summons for jury service. I cannot believe it; I totally forgot about the summons as I was deferred last November due to my going through chemotherapy. Well, they have found me and have summoned me yet again. I am due to appear in court on the Monday, October 24 for November jury service. I called them and notified them that I am unable to do it this time around as I am going through radiotherapy, fortunately they have *excused* me from jury service until further notice but were unable to *defer* me for a second time—it all sounds the same to me.

Thursday, October 23, my radiotherapy appointment was for 11:20 a.m., followed by a clinic appointment at 11:45 a.m. Every radiotherapy patient needs a weekly appointment with the clinic doctors just to check that there is no skin damage or discoloration or burning of the skin, and to generally give feedback on how they are feeling during the radiotherapy process. My weekly appointments had been set up for every Thursday, which meant spending most of the day at the hospital—what joy! Anyway, I arrived early Thursday to get my blood tested and then went down in time for radiotherapy only to be told that they were running fifteen minutes late. I did mention that I had a clinic appointment scheduled for 11:45 a.m. Needless to say, stripping is getting to be a habit with me, and I was afraid; the timing was so tight I just went straight into the treatment room and pulled down my pants and lay on the bed. No time to change into pajama bottoms—no time for formalities. They quickly zapped me, and I ran upstairs to the outpatient room to wait for my name to be called. Here is this patience again— the clinic was running thirty minutes late.

One of the nurses in the clinic weighed me, and I was absolutely horrified; I had put on +-4lbs in weight over three weeks, which was quite the shocker! I am back to my normal, pre-cancer weight. I could not believe it. Well, I could; I had not been limiting myself to anything whatsoever. If I fancied a piece of cake or late-night snack, I had been eating it. During my illness I had been eating like a pig and not been able to put on weight. Now, I know I am healed, and weight is staying on. I am weighing a hefty 128lbs but am looking back to my normal self, and that is the sign of health. I am going to stop moaning about my bum looking big and start doing something about it. I am going to try and stop eating massive portions of food and just keep walking every day to the hospital and back and keep doing everything around the house as per normal. Eating well-balanced, healthy meals and exercising are the most important factors to recovery—besides putting your absolute trust in Jesus—but that is a given.

With daily appointments and sometimes two a day at the hospital, I am finally realizing that I am not in control of anything; God is and He is the one I should lean into, not my own self. Whatever happens to me here on in, God is in control of my life and my circumstances. Late appointments, whatever, they all happen for a reason, and ultimately God knows. It sounds like a bit of a cop-out, but trust me, it is not. I have always been a very stubborn, independent woman, and for me to hand my life over to the Lord Jesus Christ and let Him do whatever He wanted with me is huge for me. I am the queen of lists, arrangements, phone calls, and so forth. I have always been in control, or so I thought—my husband would like to differ on this point, *but* thank you, Jesus, for the lessons I am learning. I am slowly feeling as if I am relinquishing my stubborn streak of intolerance and impatience—very slowly—and handing my life over to Him to have His way in my life, totally.

Thursday, November 6, I had my usual Thursday clinic appointment set up for 12:30 p.m. and my daily radiotherapy set up for 2:40 p.m. I find it amazing that the ladies on reception are able to give each radiotherapy patient a list of appointments six weeks in advance, as there are hundreds of patients to squeeze into the treatments. I arrived at the train station two hours earlier than normal as the previous day, for no apparent reason, the Epsom Downs train which stops at Belmont Station, where the RMH is, had been cancelled. I wanted to get to the train station early just to check that the train had not been cancelled again. Fortunately, on arrival, I found that it was not cancelled but delayed—not anything new, I am afraid. As a result of arriving early I found myself in the RMH Outpatient Department a whole one and a half-hours early. Fortunately I am reading the "Chronicles of Brothers," a series of books by Wendy Alec, and they are absolutely gripping, so the time flies really quickly.

While walking through the RMH gates, I was just praying to the Lord and saying how much I hated hospitals, I hated seeing the suffering, and I hated the smells. In fact I hated everything about hospitals. I was almost three weeks into my radiotherapy, and how I wished it would only be four weeks treatment, not the six weeks they finally agreed on. I was finding that the radiotherapy was starting to give me short, sharp pains on my left side, and I was becoming discolored on my pelvis. In the grand scheme of things, not a big deal at all, but the daily commute was really tiring for me. The radiotherapy treatment only took two minutes, but the commute took three hours there and back. In a way, it was getting me prepared for when I returned back to work, but it was starting to get tedious, especially with the daily delays on the train.

The clinic was running thirty minutes late which was a bit of a pain, but I finally got to see one of the doctors on the team. I mentioned the short, sharp pain I was experiencing and some bleeding, which initially was a bit disconcerting. However, she did not seem too worried about the whole episode and asked if I was on any painkillers or anti-inflammatories. Of course I said no; I hate taking tablets unless I absolutely have to. Thank the Lord, it has not seemed necessary to take such steps. She did however recommend that I start taking paracetamol, as it would alleviate the pain. The radiotherapy inflames the insides, and it would be wise to take some sort of painkiller. She did mention cocodamol, which has codeine, which of course, makes you constipated—no thanks! Overall, they seemed really pleased with my progress and then—amazing news—amazing Jesus—she queried the six weeks of treatment and said that it should be four weeks. I was blown away by God's love, care, and attention to my needs. So, instead of finishing radiotherapy on November 28, I am now finishing the treatment on the Friday, November 14—I cannot wait.

I then made my way to the RMH restaurant and killed a couple of hours reading my book and eating a sandwich and praying under my breath. I am just in awe of how much the Lord Jesus Christ cares for me, is aware of my every need, and has been with me through thick and thin, carrying me through my valley of darkness and bringing me through. The Lord is the ballast in my boat, He is the one who sustains me and guides me through my storms of life, and He is my lighthouse, the safe harbor. I know I have repeated how amazing God is throughout this book, but I just cannot help myself—accept my apologies beforehand for the repetition.

I made my 2:40 p.m. appointment with the radiographers who kindly changed the timeline of my treatments, and we had a good laugh. I had baked the doctors, receptionists, and radiographers some flapjacks, so we had a nice chat and a cup of tea over flapjacks. It is so important to thank everyone at the RMH who have dedicated their lives to the cause of ridding this earth from the curse of cancer. They are an amazing staff and very caring; I am always blown away by their smiles and love shown to the patients generally.

It was Wednesday, November 12, and I was really feeling a fair bit of pain from all the radiotherapy. Thank God, this was my fourth and last week of radio. God knew beforehand that my body could not take any more than the four weeks of radiotherapy; I am just so grateful that it is not the allotted six weeks as previously discussed.

I cannot explain the pain, but it is very unnerving. You feel as if you are carrying a football inside your stomach, and when you need to use the restroom, it feels as if your whole insides are sinking to the bottom and out into the toilet. I was walking with a stoop and holding my tummy, which looks really odd. This pain had only come about in the last week of radiotherapy, and the doctors had reassured me that it would only last for a couple weeks after completion of the treatment.

Yesterday morning, I was in a fair bit of pain, so I started taking a couple of paracetamol tablets in the morning and a couple in the evening. I had been listening to a few of Louis Giglio's sermons on "Looking up" and that is what I was doing. I was not focusing on the circumstances I find myself in, but I was ultimately trusting the Lord Jesus Christ. I found myself on my bedroom floor, kneeling in prayer but totally drenched with tears. I think

I had reached a point in the treatments where I just had enough. I know God has a plan for me in my life, but I was so very tired of everything. All I seemed to do and say seemed a struggle lately. I had to focus on the end prize, which is total healing and deliverance from this curse of cancer that Satan has put on my life. God knows the bigger picture and I put my faith and trust in Him; there is no one better. It was just such a relief to let all the built-up tears and anger flood over me and rid myself of all ill feeling. The joy of the Lord is my strength.

Thursday, November 13, both my sisters took me to the hospital for my radiotherapy treatment and my last clinic appointment. I had not wanted anyone to take me for radiotherapy, but since it was all of us triplets together, we were going to make a day of it. I had my radiotherapy, and it was a bit of a struggle lying down on the bed, and I was in a bit of discomfort. After the radiotherapy we went upstairs and waited an hour to see the doctor in the clinic. It was quite funny, as the doctor entered the room, she was not too sure who to look at, as my sisters and I were rather confusing her. She checked me out and said that everything seems as it should be. It was reassuring to hear that the pain I was experiencing was common in patients who had radiotherapy on their pelvis area for a month. She explained that the organs and nodules inside the tummy were inflamed and that I would be experiencing a fair bit of pain for the next month or so—I of course rebuked that—one week, Lord, maximum. I must say that my lower pelvis had discolored a lot and had gone quite dark, a shame they could not put the same color on my whole body. Also, I had lost all of my hair; if I only knew, I would not have bothered doing laser hair removal years prior! There is always an upside to treatments, and you have to find them and laugh about it. The doctor said I should expect some scabbing and skin irritation, but I know that is not going to happen. I am smacking on aqueous cream and trusting the Lord that whatever side effects have been mentioned are not taking place on my body.

Finally, after leaving the hospital we were all ravenous, so we decided to go and eat out really expensive—Burger King. We all had a whopper burger and chips (we did ask for the less fat ones). It was the nicest burger I have tasted in a very long time. I know; I have to get out more. Thank God, I am eating like a piggy and enjoying every mouthful. I just have to be disciplined and start eating more normal healthy portions from next week. I think it is my sisters who are corrupting me. I don't think I have had a Burger King in fifteen years or more.

On Friday, November 14, we got up really early in the morning: 4:00 a.m. My sister, Joy, was leaving on an early flight back to Brisbane in Australia. I am really going to miss having her around, but we are always skyping each other, so it is not that bad. Emil had the day off, so we went for my final radiotherapy appointment together, which was lovely. We left the RMH in Sutton around noon and made our way to RMH in Chelsea for a 3:00 p.m. appointment with Dr. Rasheed. I had baked him and his team a tin of shortbread and was really looking forward to seeing him again; it has been a while.

Emil took me to lunch, but we had to eat it really quickly in order to get to the hospital in time. We arrived at the outpatient clinic in time for my 3:00 p.m. appointment. Unfortunately, by 4:00, we were told that the clinic was still running forty-five minutes late. By this time, I was absolutely exhausted from the radiotherapy in the morning and waiting around at RMH yesterday and today, waiting to see doctors. Trust me, I am totally sympathetic to the doctors and nurses and realize they are very short staffed. I went to the clinic nurses' room and gave them the tin of shortbread for everyone to share and said that I would be leaving before I got to see Dr. Rasheed. I was very tired and if Dr. Rasheed needed to see me, then by all means, please call me for a later appointment. To be honest, I think the clinic appointment was out of courtesy. Until I have my CT scan in early January, there really is no point seeing Dr. Rasheed. I am sure Dr. Rasheed was grateful that he had one less patient to see on a late Friday afternoon.

My next appointment with the radiotherapy team is on December 15, 2014, which is supposed to be my first day back at the office, never mind; it cannot be helped. My first appointment with the colorectal team is on January 12, 2015. I believe I will have to have a CT scan in the interim, to see if everything is clear. I cannot wait for the day to hear that I have the all clear. It seems like a dream I cannot imagine can come true.

I have been on such a mental rollercoaster the past eighteen months that it is very hard to explain to people. On the one hand, you are on a high hearing you have the all clear, and the next minute being told your tumor markers are up or that they were unable to take everything out during surgery. But, I can honestly say, that through the darkest of days, not knowing if I would pull through or not, the Lord Jesus Christ has never left my side. I have experienced such joy and peace that has flooded the very depths of my soul; it is an amazing buzz you get from putting all your cares and burdens onto Him. So, I am bending my knees and looking up.

It is now a couple of weeks after radiotherapy finished, and I am finally starting to feel normal again. Ignorance is bliss, and before every treatment I have to go through I never have wanted to know what the treatments entail. I had found out that my insides were inflamed through radio, and while I had sailed through the first three weeks of radiotherapy, I did find the fourth week quite intense. I was struggling to walk upright with a good posture, and I was experiencing pain from my inflamed organs. It felt like I was carrying a brick around inside me. Thank God it only lasted a couple of weeks and now I am feeling great. Throughout my treatment I was still walking wherever I needed to go, still eating like a piggy, and still leading as normal life as possible.

Also, radiation has discolored my skin to a lovely dark tan, it is such a shame it is not staying as I have now started to peel and am losing the lovely skin tone. Although it does look a bit odd, that it is in just one place so maybe it's just as well. I have also just received a letter in the mail from the hospital, requesting me to come in for the CT scan on January 2, 2015, along with blood tests to see where my tumor markers are. I am excited to go to my clinic appointment on January 12, and hear the results of the scan. I have no doubt whatsoever that my Maker has my life in His hands and that His will shall be done.

Chapter Sixteen

Back to Work

J am very excited to return back to work on Monday, December 15, and have something to focus my energies on. It may sound silly but for the past month I have been trying to go to bed early, around 10:00 p.m. and wake up when the alarm goes off at 5:00 a.m. and actually get up and get dressed and start doing my daily chores. I find that it is helping me get back into the swing of things easily, and my body clock is adjusting far easier as well. I have to say, however, when I do get to bed, I find that my mind is so active that I do struggle to get a full six hours of sleep a night. To be honest, I have never been a very sound sleeper throughout my life, but I was hoping this might change. It does seem like I am slowly getting back to normal, which is not a bad thing. After working in the city of London for over twenty years and getting up at 5:00 in the morning and not sleeping much, it is part of my DNA.

Fortunately, God has blessed me with amazing jobs, and I have loved each and every one of them, so there is no room to complain.

On December 9, my work Christmas party will take place at one of my work colleague's house, so it is a great opportunity to see everyone before I start work the following week. It is just a shame I have a clinic appointment the very first day I am back in the office on the Monday, December 15.

Change of plan: I start work on Tuesday, December 16, as I have to attend the clinic on December 15, which is such an inconvenience. I cannot tell you throughout this illness, what an inconvenience the whole thing has been. I am seriously getting annoyed with hospitals, clinic appointments, and needles!

On Monday, December 15, I arrived at RMH at 3:00 p.m. for my radiotherapy clinic appointment. Unfortunately, I had to give blood first, as I had received in the mail an envelope with some test tubes in from the Genetics Faculty in Oxford requesting I partake in some genetics trials. I am more than happy to help future generations fight the curse of cancer so, as you know, me and needles do not go well, but I was happy to comply. Fortunately, there is a lovely man in the lab who allows me to "stab and go." This means that he is very fast, no messing around; he stabs you with the needle and you are out of the lab within minutes—I love it! No messing around with unwrapping the needle, rubbing the solution on your arm, and so forth. As the advertisement says, "Just Do It."

After giving blood, I went back to the outpatient waiting room and waited my turn to see a clinic doctor. Fortunately, the doctor in the radiotherapy team saw me within minutes, which was great. The doctor seemed really pleased with my progress; the discoloration of my skin was lightening, and the swelling in my tummy was markedly down. So thank you, Jesus, for bringing me through radiotherapy without any setbacks or permanent effects. The doctor mentioned that I would be having a CT scan on January 2, and before I went to the scanning department on that day, I would need to go to the lab and have some more blood taken—hooray, more needles.

Fortunately, I finished at the clinic early enough to walk fast down the hill to Belmont train station, and the train arrived within minutes of my arrival on the platform. I arrived home and was absolutely buzzing as I would go back to work the next day. I laid out my clothes for the following day, set the alarm, and waited for my lovely husband, Emil, to arrive back from work so we could eat dinner together.

My first week back at work was amazing. Everyone seemed really pleased to see me back, but I think it was because they all missed my baking—that's a joke. It was a relaxing week as you can imagine; it was the last week in the office with everyone before they all fly off to their respective families in France and the United States. We shared a lovely team lunch together on the Friday, December 19, and we all had a really good laugh. I still have to pinch myself; I cannot believe I am back to relative normalcy and back among amazing colleagues and friends.

Monday, December 22, had not started well for commuting up to London Bridge. For the next two weeks, all trains from East Croydon to London Bridge were not running due to major engineering works. I had to go to London Blackfriars and walk twenty-five minutes to work—actually not such a bad idea as it gave me my exercise with a purpose. Unfortunately, on the way back home in the evening, there were no District and Circle Lines operating between Embankment and Victoria so I had to get off at Embankment and take the Bakerloo line to Oxford Circus and then the Victoria line to the Victoria overground station. That's not so bad but just added a further half hour to my journey, and needless to say, I do not enjoy the underground as I feel so claustrophobic. So, if anyone is reading this book and wants to come to London over Bank Holidays then I would encourage you not to; this is the time when Network Rail decides to do major upgrades to the network.

My brother, Ian, who lives in South Africa, was to arrive in London on Saturday, December 20; it was a last minute surprise, and we were both very excited to have him with us for Christmas. Emil's mom and dad were to arrive in the UK from Los Angeles for Christmas on December 23; we were going to have a full house and were really looking forward to it. We would spend Christmas day with Ian and the folks, and then on Boxing Day, we would have my whole family join us. There should be around fifteen people celebrating with us over "bubble and squeak." I love Christmas time and what it represents. I am not too sure if most of the secular world really knows the true meaning, but for us Christians, it is to celebrate the birth of Jesus. God sending his only beloved son on earth was the beginning of our redemption. Jesus' sole purpose for coming to earth was to die for us in order that we may be redeemed and set free—amen. Jesus was our present at Christmas.

On New Year's Day, 2015, I was absolutely exhausted. I had been working throughout, and we had also been entertaining a lot, so today I decided to take it easy. Emil's folks were with us, and they were to leave on January 6. The night before, we saw some amazing fireworks all around Surrey and London. From our fifteenth-floor apartment we had a bird's eye view of Surrey, and some of the fireworks on display were breath-taking, including the River Thames and London Eye fireworks. So, we had the luxury of staying in our warm flat and being able to see the displays all around us in the comfort of our own home—lovely.

The next day, Friday, January 2, at 10:25 I needed to have my CT scan and bloods. I was planning to be in the office for the afternoon and try and get everything ship-shape before the team gets back into the office on Monday. Those past two weeks at work had been lovely. I had time to get expenses done and try to sort out all the various board meetings for the forthcoming year, in order that no clashes would occur. It is rather depressing, working out an A3 piece of paper with your boss's movements on them for the following year. It had only been Frank, the receptionist, and me in the office, and we had a good laugh and a couple of pub lunches while everyone was away.

I arrived early at RMH in order to have my blood drawn. God, how I hate the smell and sight of hospitals. On January 2, 2015, back at the hospital, it seemed as if nothing had changed. There were the same old illnesses, the same old people, and the same old issues. The curse of cancer completely takes over peoples' lives and messes up their whole psych. Thank you, Jesus, for your precious blood that covers me all the time. I gave my blood and moved up to the first floor for my CT scan. I forgot that my left arm is better for injections, but I had already given my vein to the lab, so the nurse contemplated re-injecting the whole. Fortunately, she found a vein in my right arm and a large cannula was inserted relatively easily. She had to make sure I was not wearing any wiring whatsoever, and then I lay on the table nice and relaxed while the scan was taking place. I could taste the iron from the dye they were injecting, but fortunately I had a pack of mints in my handbag to use afterward. It was a nice relaxing morning, and I arrived at the office around 1:00 p.m., in time for lunch! I had to buck my ideas up and start getting things in order before the office personnel arrived back on Monday, January 5. It was the last day of just Frank and me in the office, I will miss the special funny moments we had, but I was also really looking forward to catching up with everyone.

We waited to see if I had the all clear or not. I have to be back at the Marsden for a clinic appointment on Monday, January 12, and I knew that the peace of the Lord my Savior would be upon me until then. I was so relaxed about the outcome because at the back of my mind I was longing for the day when I would see the Lord face to face. That is when I will have a perfect body, and there are no more tears or pain. Heaven is real, and heaven is waiting for every one of us. I can't wait! May the Lord's will be done in my life.

On Monday, January 12, Emil and I left the office around 1:00 p.m. and made our way slowly towards Victoria Station in order to get the train to Belmont Station. It was not a big surprise that the train departing from London Victoria was late, and we managed to arrive just in time at Marsden Hospital for my blood work and the clinic appointment. It is never a good sign when one of the doctors in the colorectal team come into the room along with one of the clinical workers. Unfortunately, my suspicions were correct. The doctor explained that my tumor markers were up and that the CT scan was inconclusive. There was suspicious shading on the margin lines and that I would need a PET scan to see exactly what was going on and how active the tumors are.

When I sat in the meeting it felt like the movie *Groundhog Day*. It was exactly the same scenario as the last time, and my heart sank. The doctor tried to remain positive and reassured me that when I came back for another clinic appointment in a couple of weeks' time, after the PET scan, they would have a clearer idea on future steps forward.

I left the hospital with a clinic appointment made for January 26, and now I had to wait for a letter from the hospital for when my PET scan would take place. That would have to take place before the clinic appointment, so it was really annoying having to take time off work, just when I was getting back into the swing of things.

Emil and I made our way slowly home again very down in the dumps. At the back of my mind, to be honest, I envied those cancer patients who died quickly. I think, after all I had been through and the waiting game for the last eighteen months, I wish my Father in heaven had taken me home when I was told initially I could have died within twenty-four hours if my tumor had burst within my colon. I was just very tired and emotionally drained. One minute being up and the next minute down with conflicting news really takes it out of you.

I received a hospital letter in the mail, notifying me of my PET scan for January 21. Fortunately, it was an afternoon appointment at the Marsden in Chelsea, which is ideal for me to get to on the underground from work. I was going to have to tell my boss that I had to take time off for the two appointments scheduled for later in January. I know they wouldn't mind, as I am sure everyone is surprised that I am even at work. I can only say, but by the grace of God, I am able to go to work with relative ease and pain free. Except for the horrible train commute to and from the city of London, everything is fine. London

Bridge was going through major construction repairs and expansion, so apparently until 2018 there would be major disruptions—something to look forward to!

I had been at work just over three weeks and was loving every moment of getting back into the swing of things. I still did not go to the gym in the mornings, which was a huge shame, but I was walking every day to and from the train station and work. It is better than nothing and during that time I had my iPod on, playing Christian music and just praying for God's grace to get me through the day ahead. I am sure the people around me must have thought that whatever I was playing, they would have liked to hear it; I can't stop smiling when I hear uplifting Christian music. I was, at the time, really into Bethel Music; the words were so uplifting and just what I needed first thing in the morning.

The one concern I had when I took a packed train or if I was in a confined space is that my stoma makes a noise, if you know what I mean. It can get awfully embarrassing, and I have found myself a couple of times pretending I did not hear anything. I have also unfortunately been full of "hot air" in the office and had to make my apologies. This is unfortunately one of the downsides I have to had to live with. Sometimes you wish the earth under you could just swallow you up, but I needed to deal with this.

Most nights I got home around 6:30 p.m., and I left the house around 6:30 a.m., so it is a full day and I found I was getting really tired. When I got home, I made myself a cup of mint tea and indulged in a couple of biscuits, sitting in bed and watching TV. TBN UK Christian TV had just come to the UK. It was long overdue and a very welcome addition to the secular TV we have on our channels. All the favorites like Joyce Meyer, Joseph Prince, Creflo Dollar, and Jesse DuPlantis are on, and it has been a real blessing watching after a long day at the office.

I must be honest and say I have been down of late, just getting really frustrated and annoyed and thinking what an inconvenience this illness has been—so many hospital visits, so many needles, and so many scans. At this stage, I was not negative and I definitely had not given up, but I so longed for heaven. I did not want to be remembered for "hanging on for dear life" or "she fought a good fight." Trust me, there is nothing to hang on to in this world, and there is only one race I want to win, as the Apostle Paul describes it. I have been reading a book written by Kat Kerr called *Revealing Heaven* and also a book written by Wendy Alec called *Visions from Heaven*. Wow! They have been truly amazing and utterly revealing as to the glory that awaits the redeemed. So many times we sing in church "When we all get to heaven, what a day of rejoicing that will be," and it will be—but why do so many Christians want to hang on to life if it is in God's plan for his redeemed to go home? I cannot wait to have a body that is perfect, no more "pooh bag" (colostomy) on me, no more scars, no more skin discoloration, and no more pain. So my dilemma is how I should pray. I have a gorgeous husband who loves me and a loving family on earth, who, I hope, would miss me terribly. But yet, I find myself drawn to my Heavenly Father who created me and who sustains me and who died for me and who loves me unconditionally. My gracious Father in Heaven has prepared a mansion for me for all eternity. So as a born-again believer, I am in a win-win situation. How do I pray, Lord Jesus?

On the one hand, I want to see my work colleagues and some family members and friends come to know my Heavenly Father by seeing a mighty miraculous healing in my body and that His name may be glorified and honored through all of this. On the other hand, I want to go home and see my earthly father and my heavenly Father and those loved ones who have gone before, including the baby I miscarried. Trust me; if anyone reading this book has miscarried or aborted a baby, they are waiting for you in heaven. So, there is so much to be excited about. These days, I find myself praying that God's will be done in my life. He has plans and a purpose in my life I do not know about. I just pray that the Lord Jesus Christ may use me all the days I have on this earth to lift up His holy name.

On Wednesday, January 21, I left the office around lunchtime and made my way to the Royal Marsden in Chelsea for my PET scan. Before having a PET scan, you are not allowed to eat for six hours beforehand and only drink water. Trust me, with my appetite, I will be famished and as for just drinking water—uuuggghhhh! Unfortunately, I am one of those people who don't enjoy just drinking water; I always have to put a drop of cordial in my water just to make it drinkable. I arrived at RMH at 2:30 p.m., which was half an hour before my appointed time as I wanted them to put Ametop cream where they were going to put the cannula. I always try and remember to ask for Ametop cream or spray, which is an anesthetic that helps relieve the pain of injections. You know me; I hate needles! I always find myself with sweaty palms before someone tries to find the vein, so this definitely does help. I don't always remember to ask for Ametop, which is to my detriment I have to admit later.

I had a lovely Ghanaian Christian gentleman do the injection, and we had a lovely chat about the Lord Jesus Christ. I love it when I go to hospital, and I have another brother or sister in the Lord helping me out—what a blessing. Once the radioactive dye was inside me, they left me for an hour in a dark room. Funny things go through your mind lying there thinking of absolutely nothing. This was my third PET scan, and I hoped it was the last. Here I was thinking, if I have radiation in me, can they see me glowing in the dark? The radioactive chemical they inject into the vein is similar to naturally occurring glucose, and it will show how cancerous tissues process glucose, how far a cancer has spread, and if it is responding to treatment.

I tried to catch a quick nap, but with all the noise outside the room it was virtually impossible. When I went through the scanning machine, it was lovely and relaxing. It only lasted thirty minutes, and it was a relief to get off the table. I have to say, throughout the whole scanning process all I could think about was food. It was almost nine hours since I had eaten last, and I was so hungry I could have eaten a horse. Fortunately, I had packed a sandwich in my bag for afterward. I left the hospital just after 5:00 p.m. and walked to the underground station eating my sandwich. To be honest, at this stage I was so hungry I just did not care about etiquette or anything else. I was also relieved to hear that I had lost 6.6lbs since my last weigh in. I was getting to be a real porker, eating loads and not exercising, so it was great news to hear I had actually lost weight. I can't say I could see it, but I was very relieved.

So now we had to wait until Monday, January 26, when we would get the results and see what lay ahead. Dear Lord Jesus, whatever happens, I put my trust in you and know that you are a good God who is able to do all good things.

Emil and I arrived on Monday, January 26, for my clinic appointment at 5:30 p.m. Unfortunately, due to a backlog of patients, we only got to see the colorectal team at 6:40 p.m. At one stage they were switching off the reception lights, and we were getting a little concerned they had forgotten us.

Finally, we were called and got to see one of the doctors on the team, along with Ramani, my clinical nurse. It was great news, and I was really excited to see how God's unfailing love and grace had been fulfilled. The PET scan came back, and it showed that the tumor markers had leveled off over the past month. Also, the worrying images that came up near the margins were due to the radiotherapy treatment. This meant that there is scarring and nothing more. Unfortunately, there was a little bit of a shadow in the middle they are not too sure of, so it required another scan to be done. However, I did not need to go back to the clinic for another three months. So thank you Jesus, no more hospitals for a while. It became a wait-and-see game, but I was fully confident in my Lord Jesus. So then I waited for the letter to come from the hospital alerting me to my scan date.

Psalm 13 has been the bible passage which has come to mean a lot to me:

> How long, O LORD? Will you forget me forever?
> How long will you hide your face from me?
> ² How long must I take counsel in my soul
> and have sorrow in my heart all the day?
> How long shall my enemy be exalted over me?
>
> ³ Consider and answer me, O LORD my God;
> light up my eyes, lest I sleep the sleep of death,

⁴lest my enemy say, "I have prevailed over him,"
lest my foes rejoice because I am shaken.

⁵**But** I have trusted in your steadfast love;
my heart shall rejoice in your salvation.
⁶I will sing to the LORD,
because he has dealt bountifully with me

People may be a little surprised by my choice of bible passage as it is not the usual Psalm 91. I just found that this Psalm demonstrates the desperation David found himself in, not too dissimilar to what I found, and how, through it all, the Lord has been amazingly good to me.

Chapter Seventeen

Wrap Up

*T*his is the final chapter, and I thank the Lord Jesus Christ that I am able to write this with my healing a foregone conclusion. The whole aim of writing this book was to give encouragement to other cancer patients. The following are a few pointers for those who have not been to a hospital before:

- Many reception areas and clinics in the hospitals have posters of various statistics concerning the death rates in cancer patients, the signs to look out for, the percentage of survivors, and so forth. I cannot think of anything worse to hang up in a reception area while waiting to go and see the doctors. I would encourage all patients to not look at these posters but to bring a good book and focus all your energy on that, or something else. These posters are only what man says, not what God says.

- When you do go for various scans and tests take a pair of slippers with you so that you can walk from the changing rooms to the scanning table and back again in comfortable slippers and not with your bare feet.

- I used to take pajama bottoms with me every day to radiotherapy, and I could keep my top half with my normal clothes on. See what you can bring to wear instead of those sexy hospital gowns.

- Ladies, try and remember not to wear zippers, underwire bras, or jewelry when you go for scans; it is really annoying trying to fit all this in your handbag afterwards.

- Try and sit as close to the reception desk as possible on arrival at the hospital outpatient clinic; not all of the nurses who shout out the names of patients have loud voices, and you may miss hearing yours.

- Always bring a bottle of water with you to your hospital visits. You need to keep hydrated, and it does help to have liquids in you when you need a needle. Water helps the veins bulge out, and it is easier for the nurses to find the vein.

- When you go to the lab to relinquish some of the red stuff, make sure you grab a ticket number when you arrive. There is a ticket number machine—something like a supermarket cheese counter.

Don't forget; otherwise you will be waiting for a very long time.

- Always be courteous and smile to the hospital staff. I cannot believe that some patients can be unbelievably abusive towards them. In fact, if you have the energy, bake something and bring it in. It always brings a smile and a lot of appreciation.

- If you do have to go through chemo, make sure you wrap up in layers. Chemo patients feel the cold, and their hands are particularly sensitive. Take a pair of gloves and thick socks.

- It is helpful to carry some mints or sweets with you; sometimes you do feel faint and a bit of sugar boosts the energy levels. You sometimes need to visualize yourself as a long distance runner and take on board some of their preparations like bananas and so forth.

- When you have to stay in hospital for a period of time, don't forget your toothbrush and shampoo. Those two things were a lifesaver for me. I felt like a new woman when I brushed my teeth and washed my hair. Dry, spray shampoo does not work!

- Once you are diagnosed, do not Google anything about your illness. Ignorance is bliss, and I totally believe in that. The element of surprise for treatments is great, you have no preconceived idea what they are going to do, and invariably, it is not as bad as you think.

- Always wear comfortable clothes and loose sleeves as it is easier to give blood rolling them up. You spend hours in the hospital at one stretch so be comfortable and warm.
- Pray that the blood of Jesus covers you before you enter the hospital as some of the sights, particularly children fighting cancer, is heart-breaking.
- Whatever the doctors say in clinic, if it is negative, rebuke it in your mind. Doctors, I have found, give out the worst-case scenario. As children of God, we need to know that while we wait, God is working. Full healing in His time—not ours.
- Always try and arrange early appointments for the clinics, as invariably they run late. The later in the day the appointment, the longer the wait.
- Imagine yourself healthy. I know this is a really tough one, especially when you are in the middle of treatment. Trust me; it does help you focus on the end results. Dare to believe in a long and strong life ahead.

Positives to Cancer

kay, believe it or not, there are some positives to cancer.

- If you have suffered from hay fever in the past, it disappears for a number of years after cancer treatment.
- You can eat like a piggy and never put on weight.
- Better, more luscious hair grows back for chemo patients who lose their hair.
- Apparently, chemo patients' feet become soft as babies bottoms, even when they started out with hard skin on their feet.
- Once you are on NHS records and a cancer patient, you get the best care available in the world for free. God bless the NHS (24 years of paying tax I now know where it goes).
- Aftercare at home is fantastic. Every month, I get a box delivered free of charge with my stoma bags, wipes, and sprays—fantastic.

- As a cancer patient, for five years after diagnosis, you are entitled to free NHS prescriptions—amazing.
- Initially, your skin shows the strains of the medication, but after everything has died down, I find my skin is a lot better/firmer than what it was before. Also, drinking a lot of liquids helps.
- If you have to go through radiotherapy then you will lose the hair on the area targeted. No need for laser hair removal—if only I knew that earlier.
- You get all the sympathy available, it seems to be all about me, myself, and I. In this instance, it is not always a bad thing. Just make sure you are humble in the process.
- If you are diagnosed with cancer, make sure your first port of call is Jesus Christ. He will give you the joy and peace to sustain you throughout your ordeal—you will need Him.

I have just received a letter from RMH to alert me about my next clinic appointment which is scheduled for Monday, April 2015. I cannot believe it, no more hospitals for a very long time, I am so excited. My PET scan is scheduled for April 21, 2015.

Throughout my illness and when this curse of Satan invaded my body, I did not dare believe that I could get my life back to as normal as possible. After having been told I had Stage 4 cancer of the ovaries and colon and then two subsequent cancer tumors, I can only say that I live today by the grace of God. I am leading as full a life as I previously had. I am back in full-time employment, I am exercising and building up my strength slowly, and I am still eating loads. I need to make a mental note to cut down on my food portions, or I will definitely start looking like a lollipop lady.

Unfortunately, I will have to live with my colostomy, but that is a very small price to pay. In some bizarre way, the long scar running vertically down my front and the colostomy is a reminder of what I have been through, and how God has brought me through, a better person for it. I am more in love with my Father in heaven than ever before, I am a stronger person, but I am also a more sympathetic person to other people's needs. I cannot explain to you what a comfort He has been in my darkest hours lying in hospital. I have sometimes felt abandoned and forgotten, but I soon snap out of that rubbish thinking and lean into my Lord. The absolute peace and joy He has always furnished me with is amazing. I still am trusting in my Savior for complete healing and a reversal, but I know that one day I will have a perfect body for eternity. This one I have here on earth is only temporary: an old, scarred, worn-out tent.

I would encourage those cancer sufferers who are going through their darkest times to never give up and to look up! It is so easy for other people to say it, but I have been there. It is not easy; sometimes I felt like giving up and asking, "What is the point?" There is a point; as Christians we are supposed to live an abundant life, filled with blessings. Our cup should be full and not just full but running over with the blessings and anointing of God. You have a choice in life: Live for the moment with joy, or live with despair and anger. I know what path I choose.

We are heirs of God and joint heirs with Christ, we are sons and daughters of the most-high God, and we are blessed and highly favored among men. The God of creation loved us so much that He forsook his Godly realm to come to earth. His sole purpose in doing this was to die and save a sinner like me. How amazing, how loving, how merciful is the Lord Jesus Christ. Surely, the least I can do is follow Him daily.

I pray that everyone who reads this book may experience just a little bit of what the Lord means to me. I pray that you may find Him, too, that you may come to love him and have a personal relationship with Him. He longs for us to talk to Him, pray with Him, sing to Him, and just call on Him in good times and bad times.

God bless and keep you all as we wait upon the
return of our Lord Jesus Christ.
Come Lord Jesus, come and take your
waiting people home.